P9-DDA-286

The Marriage of a Marquis

DISCARD

DEWITT COMMUNITY LIBRARY
SHOPPINGTOWN MALL
3649 ERIE BLVD. EAST
DEWITT, NEW YORK 13214

JUL 21 2013

Publications of the North American Jules Verne Society

The Palik Series (edited by Brian Taves)

The Marrriage of a Marquis (*The Marriage of Mr. Anselme des Tilleuls* and *Jédédias Jamet, or The Tale of an Inheritance*)
   Contributors: Edward Baxter, Jean-Michel Margot, Walter James Miller, Kieran M. O'Driscoll, Brian Taves

Shipwrecked Family: Marooned with Uncle Robinson
   Translated by Sidney Kravitz

The Count of Chanteleine: A Tale of the French Revolution
   Translated by Edward Baxter; Notes by Garmt de Vries-Uiterweed, Volker Dehs

Stories by Jules and Michel Verne (*Fact-Finding Mission, Pierre-Jean*, and *The Fate of Jean Morénas*)
   Translated, with notes, by Kieran M. O'Driscoll

Historical Novels: *San Carlos* and *The Siege of Rome*
   Translated by Edward Baxter

(Other volumes in preparation)

The North American Jules Verne Society also copublished (with Prometheus)

Journey Through the Impossible
   Translated by Edward Baxter; Notes by Jean-Michel Margot

Editorial Committee of the North American Jules Verne Society:

Henry G. Franke III   Dr. Terry Harpold
Jean-Michel Margot   Dr. Brian Taves
          Professor Walter James Miller

The Marriage of a Marquis

The Palik Series

Contributors:
Edward Baxter
Jean-Michel Margot
Walter James Miller
Kieran M. O'Driscoll
Brian Taves

Edited by Brian Taves for the North American Jules Verne Society

BearManor Fiction

2011

DEWITT COMMUNITY LIBRARY

The Marriage of a Marquis
by Jules Verne
© 2011 North American Jules Verne Society

All rights reserved.

For information, address:

BearManor Fiction
P. O. Box 71426
Albany, GA 31708

bearmanormedia.com

North American Jules Verne Society: najvs.org

Cover design from an original 19th century French edition

Typesetting and layout by John Teehan

Published in the USA by BearManor Media

ISBN—1-59393-361-4
978-1-59393-361-6

Table of Contents

Foreword: The Mission of the Palik Series 1
   by Brian Taves

Introduction: The Rehabilitation of Jules Verne
   in America—From Boy's Author to Adult's Author,
   1960-2010 11
   by Walter James Miller

Jules Verne's Humor: A Portfolio of Original
   French Engravings 23

Preface: The Marriage of Mr. Anselme des Tilleuls 41
   by Jean-Michel Margot

The Marriage of Mr. Anselme des Tilleuls by Jules Verne 51
   Translated by Edward Baxter
   Notes by Jean-Michel Margot

Afterword: The Tribulations of a Translator Of Jules Verne 83
   by Edward Baxter

Appendix: Jédédias Jamet, or The Tale of an Inheritance 91
   An unfinished novel by Jules Verne
   Translated, and with a Preface and Annotations,
   by Kieran M. O'Driscoll

Contributors 121

To Edward D. Palik,

*fellow North American Jules Verne Society
member and benefactor, who had a
special interest in bringing Verne stories
previously unavailable in English
to readers.*

*We dedicate the first volume
of the Palik Series to his memory.*

Jules Verne at the height of his fame.

The Mission of the Palik Series

by Brian Taves

This volume continues the endeavor of the North American Jules Verne Society to offer readers the highest-quality translations of Verne works previously overlooked by English-language publishers. The North American Jules Verne Society is fortunate in the bequest of one of our members, Edward D. Palik, who has made possible a series dedicated to this goal. Toward this end we have assembled scholars and translators, "the Jules Verne rescue team," as we have been dubbed by our dean, Walter James Miller.

That a Verne rescue mission needs to be undertaken in the United States might seem paradoxical. "Father Jules" (as Isaac Asimov labeled him in his foreword to the 1965 combination volume, *20,000 Leagues Under the Sea and Around the Moon*) has been America's best-loved French author for generations. Yet, even at the beginning of the 1990s, Verne's reputation here could have best been paraphrased in the words of one of his favorite writers, Charles Dickens. Verne was the best known of authors, and the worst known of authors.

Verne's reputation had been damaged in the English-speaking world during his lifetime (1828-1905) and beyond by poor translations. For 30 years, from 1869 to 1898, his books were rushed into publication for a 19th century mass market, often in pirated editions. In the years to come, the worst of these renderings would become the most often reprinted.

Even before Verne's death, publishers increasingly refused to present his ideas, unfiltered, to English speaking readers. The often downbeat writer, warning of science's potentially detrimental impact on society, was diluted into a cheerful patron saint of technological advancement. Although one or more Verne titles continued to be published annually in France until 1910, after 1898 only two appeared simultaneously in English. The reason was not commercial: sales of Verne books remained profitable in Britain and the United States, as indicated by the steady issuing of new editions of such minor novels as *Claudius Bombarnac* (1892). Even after World War I, through the late 1920s, Sampson Low continued to reprint many of the lesser known Verne works.

During the 1880s, Verne stories had become mainstays of *The Boy's Own Paper* in England, and American publishers came to rely more and more on utilizing the English translations, rather than commissioning fresh ones for use in the United States. In turn, British publishers were fearful of offending their readers in the empire, because Verne's later novels were more daring in their themes, particularly in portraying colonial depredations. Censorship grew beyond simply changing or removing controversial passages, to effectively suppressing the books by simply not translating them into English. The caution was such that *Le Testament d'un excentrique* (*The Will of an Eccentric*, 1899), Verne's last story set entirely in the United States, which appeared in England in 1900, was not published in America until 2009.

Yet the fascination with Verne in the United States was an emotion fully reciprocated by the author, who offered American characters or settings in over a third of his novels. To Verne, the United States represented the confidence of Yankee ingenuity, and the sincerity of his interest is demonstrated by the fact that he had already used this country as a setting in *De la Terre à la Lune* (*From the Earth to the Moon*, 1865) and *Les Forceurs de blocus* (*The Blockade Runners*, 1865) before his books had been largely discovered through English-language translation. Indeed, prior to age 20, he had begun *Jédédias Jamet, or The Tale of an Inheritance*, a novel intended to take place partly in this country. (Given this fact, along with its stylistic similarity to *The Marriage of Mr. Anselme des Tilleuls*, *Jédédias Jamet* has been included as an appendix to this volume.) Verne's only trip to the United States was in the spring of 1867, when he was virtually unknown here, although his books were already bestsellers in France.

The first group of Verne enthusiasts was formed, ironically, not in France, but in England. The Jules Verne Confederacy began in 1921 at Dartmouth Royal Naval College, publishing *Nautilus*, a literary magazine in tribute to Verne and his son Michel. The most permanent legacy of the Confederacy was in the publication of the Everyman's Library edition of *Five Weeks in a Balloon and Around the World in Eighty Days* in England by J.M. Dent & Sons in 1926. G.N. Pocock, the former instructor and advisor of the "Julians" (as the teenagers called themselves), had married and left Dartmouth for a second career in publishing. Pocock secured an introduction from the leaders of the Confederacy, K.B. Meiklem and A. Chancellor. Their introduction, the best critical overview on Verne in English up to that time, contains one of the first comprehensive bibliographies of editions in English, noting translators. The Confederacy must have known of the issue, because both *Cinq semaines en ballon* (*Five Weeks in a Balloon*, 1863) and *Le Tour du monde en quatre-vingts jours* (*Around the World in Eighty Days*, 1873) were newly rendered into quality translations for this edition. The influence of this volume far outlasted its time, remaining in print for forty years.

A similar but longer-lasting effort took place on the other side of the Atlantic with the American Jules Verne Society. It began when Willis E. Hurd penned an article, "A Collector and His Jules Verne," for the August 1936 issue of *Hobbies* magazine. Hurd recounted his discovery that most of Verne's novels available in English had received many different translations, often drastically edited and with widely divergent titles. Hurd's retirement allowed him to take an interest in authoring English versions of some of Verne's untranslated stories, including "Gil Braltar" (1887) in 1938.

The history of Verne studies in the English language has paralleled the evolution of translations. During Verne's lifetime, newspapers and magazines in many languages offered numerous articles (many of them wildly inaccurate), interviews, and countless reviews celebrating his new form of scientific romance. The initial book in English, *Jules Verne* by Kenneth Allott, was a 1940 critical study that sought to place Verne in the cultural and social context of such 19th century literary movements as romanticism and positivism. By contrast, the first purely biographical work on Verne came three years later with *Jules Verne: The Biography of an Imagination*, by George H. Waltz, an associate editor of *Popular Mechanics*. Waltz uncovered some obscure information, but his lack of footnotes leaves the reader uncertain where his research ended and his own imagination began.

By 1953, Americans anticipated the Europeans, and Stanford L. Luce, Jr., completed the first doctoral dissertation on Verne, at Yale. Some fifteen years later, a new Verne organization began with the Dakkar Grotto, named after the final resting place of Captain Nemo and the *Nautilus* in *L'Île mystérieuse* (*The Mysterious Island*, 1875). This association resulted in two issues of a journal entitled *Dakkar* between 1967 and 1968. Americans again set a precedent for European Verne scholarship in the 1970s with Walter James Miller's "Annotated Jules Verne" series.

By the 1980s, three doctoral dissertations, one in the United States and two in England, resulted in a series of books. From America came *Jules Verne Rediscovered: Didacticism and the Scientific Novel* (1988) by Arthur B. Evans, who discussed the ideological and semiotic aspects of Verne's works, emphasizing their pedagogical purposes. From across the Atlantic, Andrew Martin's *The Knowledge of Ignorance: From Genesis to Jules Verne* (1985) and *The Mask of the Prophet: The Extraordinary Fictions of Jules Verne* (1990), examined Verne's interaction with a number of political and literary trends of the 19th century. William Butcher authored *Verne's Journey to the Centre of the Self: Space and Time in the "Voyages Extraordinaires"* (1990), followed by *Jules Verne: The Definitive Biography* (2006). A distinctly Anglo-American school of Verne studies had developed.

The Jules Verne Encyclopedia began to take shape in the late 1980s, the brainchild of Stephen Michaluk, whom I joined as editor and coauthor. In addition to a comprehensive bibliography of all the Verne editions and translations, we sought to indicate precisely which Verne stories awaited publication in English. No one previously had undertaken this basic bibliographic exercise, and not since the Fitzroy editions of I.O. Evans, two decades earlier, had a never-before translated story appeared in English, and *The Jules Verne Encyclopedia* (finally published in 1996) helped to change this.

Evelyn Copeland, a retired French teacher and personal friend, became interested in one of these, *Aventures de la famille Raton* (*Adventures of the Rat Family*). I persuaded Oxford University Press to publish it as a separate book in 1993, using the color illustrations from the story's original appearance in *Le Figaro illustré* in1891—the first time they were all reproduced in any language. My afterword to *Adventures of the Rat Family* explored why it and other Verne stories, such as "The Humbug" (included in *The Jules Verne Encyclopedia*) had not yet appeared in English. Both *Adventures of the Rat Family* and "The Humbug" dealt with evolution, and the anxiety over Darwinism had provided sufficient motive for editorial avoidance, a thesis validated since by the rise of "creationism."

Several university presses brought fresh translations of Verne classics, including a number of versions of *Vingt Mille Lieues sous les mers* (*Twenty Thousand Leagues Under the Sea*, 1869). However, newly discovered books were also emerging from the archives in France. *Voyage à reculons en Angleterre et en Ecosse* (*Journey Backwards to England and Scotland*, 1862) was Verne's fictionalized account of his own trip in 1859. British interest in his depiction of their country facilitated the publication in 1992 by Chambers under the title of *Backwards to Britain*, translated by Janice Valls-Russell.

In 1994, Hachette issued Verne's *Paris au XXe Siècle* (*Paris in the 20th Century*), and numerous articles appeared in newspapers and periodicals from around the world reporting the remarkable discovery of the 1864 manuscript, reputedly in an old family safe. The book was soon appearing in the languages of the globe with as much alacrity as the books of Verne's heyday, and following the trend Random House commissioned an English version by Richard Howard, originally scheduled for 1995, and finally published in December 1996. By that time readers had largely forgotten the publicity, with the result that sales of *Paris in the 20th Century* in this country did not live up to Random House's expectations.

For all the progress made in Verne translations and critical editions, *Paris in the 20th Century* took a step back. Howard, previously familiar to Vernians for lucidly rendering into English the essays on Verne of such prominent theoreticians as Roland Barthes and Michel Butor, now described Verne as analyzed only by a few "eccentrics." In a conversation with me, after his lecture on Verne at the French Institute–Alliance Française in New York City on January 24, 1997, he vaguely described the style and liberties of 19th century translators of Verne as having a "wonderful tonality" which he sought to emulate in his approach to *Paris in the 20th Century*.

In 1993, the North American Jules Verne Society (NAJVS) formed, and has steadily grown with annual meetings and a newsletter, *Extraordinary Voyages*, that is now peer reviewed. In 2003, NAJVS underwrote the translation by Edward Baxter and arranged through Prometheus for the publication of Verne's 1882 play, *Voyage à travers l'impossible* (*Journey Through the Impossible*), the first complete edition of this science fiction theatrical spectacle in any language.

Here Verne tells a humorous story of cosmic travel to another planet in a distant galaxy. Staged to acclaim in France in 1882, *Journey Through the Impossible* was then lost for over a century; Georges Méliès had only the vaguest idea of its plot when making his 1904 film version. Verne's French editor, to whom he was contractually bound, usually rejected or toned down his true science fiction. Not only had *Paris in the Twentieth Century* been rejected outright, but the same editor compelled Verne to transform his trek around the solar system on a comet in *Hector Servadac* (1877) into simply a "dream."

By traveling to outer space through the theater, not prose, Verne found an escape from his publisher's dictums. Verne had already adapted some of his novels into theatrical hits, long before movies of his books first flickered on silent screens. *Journey Through the Impossible* went to the center of the earth and under the sea, destinations from some of his most popular novels. In the underground realms dwell Troglodytes anticipating the Morlocks of H.G. Wells's *The Time Machine* (1895). *Journey Through the Impossible* returns to the submarine *Nautilus*, with a visit to the city of Atlantis. The play includes appearances by many of the most famous characters from Verne's novels, including the evil scientist Doctor Ox and the members of the Baltimore Gun Club that launched the first projectile to the moon. Their giant cannon now dispatches a capsule of explorers to Altor, a newly-discovered distant planet with two suns. A preface and footnotes by Jean-Michel Margot explain the many allusions in *Journey Through the Impossible*, allowing the reader to imagine how it would have been experienced in the theater of 1882.

Despite this modern Anglophone Jules Verne renaissance, by the mid 1990s many Verne stories still remained to be translated into English, as well as more that had been newly discovered in France. The next step fell to Verne enthusiasts who began a series of selfless efforts, often without book contracts. Sidney Kravitz's personal enthusiasm for *The Mysterious Island* led him to compose a new translation of it. He did the same for *L'Oncle Robinson* (*Uncle Robinson*), the incomplete first draft, rejected by Verne's editor, of the book that eventually evolved, with entirely new characters, into *The Mysterious Island*.

The listing of the untranslated texts provided in *The Jules Verne Encyclopedia* pointed out what needed to be done and soon experts went to work. Edward Baxter began with *L'Invasion de la mer* (*The Invasion of the Sea*, 1905) and 40 years after his Yale dissertation on Verne, Stanford Luce undertook the first translation of *Le Superbe Orénoque* (*The Mighty Orinoco*, 1898) and *Les Frères Kip* (*The Kip Brothers*, 1902) and finished with a new translation of *Les Cinq cents millions de la Bégum* (*The The 500 Millions of the Begum*, 1879), retitled *The Begum's Millions*.

This reservoir provided a critical mass when Wesleyan University Press approached Arthur Evans to start a Classics of Science Fiction series in 2001 (which continues to this day). The untranslated "Voyages Extraordinaires" were a natural foundation, as was Kravitz's version of *The Mysterious Island* and Luce's *The Begum's Fortune*. All of these have been critical editions, with introductory material and annotations, along with the original engravings from the French editions.

An abrupt slip back occurred in 1998 when University of Nebraska Press's Bison imprint issued *The Chase of the Golden Meteor* exactly as it had first appeared in England in 1908. First on the Jules Verne Forum listserve, then in a review for the Summer 1999 issue of *Extrapolation*, I attacked this, not only because *The Chase of the Golden Meteor* was from a turn-of-the-century translation, but it was from the version of *La Chasse au météore* rewritten by Jules's son, Michel Verne. Nebraska had secured an introduction by Gregory Benford, so clearly there was an attempt to distinguish the book as something more than a reprint. Nonetheless, there was no recognition of the obvious question of the true authorship.

The Chase of the Golden Meteor had been translated from one of the nine posthumously published Verne books that were guided into print by Michel. For many years, the Verne family argued that Michel's changes did not go beyond stylistic polishing, updating, or possible verbal instructions from father to son; indeed the two had already collaborated during the father's lifetime. Jules Verne always drastically rewrote his books once he saw them in proof, often several times over, so his own manuscript versions submitted to the publisher were never equivalent to the final edition in print.

However, as the evidence of the manuscripts became public in the early 1980s, what only Verne's publisher had known at the time was now clear to all. Michel altered all the works posthumously published under his father's name from 1905 to 1914, even originating two of the books himself. The original manuscripts have been published, exposing Michel's alterations, from the addition of new characters, changing climaxes, to the revision of basic themes. Modified in such ways were *Le Phare du bout du monde* (*The Lighthouse at the End of the World*, 1905), *Le Volcan d'or* (*The Golden Volcano*, 1906), *La Chasse au météore, Le Pilote du Danube* (*The Danube Pilot*, 1908, entitled by Jules as *Le Beau Danube Jaune* [*The Beautiful Yellow Danube*]), and *Le Secret de Wilhelm Storitz* (*The Secret of Wilhelm Storitz*, 1910). Michel expanded *En Magellanie* (*Magellania*, 1987) three-fold into *Les Naufragés du Jonathan* (*The Survivors of the Jonathan*, 1910) and infused it with his own leftist political sentiments; the sympathetic treatment of the anarchist philosophy that permeates the revised novel was largely his contribution. Michel's politics were more radical, and his taste in science fiction more futuristic, than his father. Subsequently, Michel carried forward his rewriting of his father's work as a movie producer through 1920 on six major celluloid adaptations.

The Jules Verne texts of the books rewritten by Michel had been shopped around for a number of years by agents for the Verne estate, but there were no takers until a small press, Welcome Rain, published *Magellania*, translated by Benjamin Ivry in 2002. At that point, Nebraska, regretting *The Chase of the Golden Meteor*, decided to follow Welcome Rain's lead with a series of critical editions. The Frederick Paul Walter and Walter James Miller translation of Jules Verne's version of *La Chasse au météore*, this time entitled *The Meteor Hunt*, appeared in 2006, followed by William Butcher's *Lighthouse at the End of the World* in 2007, and Edward Baxter's *The Golden Volcano* in 2008, with *The Secret of Wilhelm Storitz* by Peter Schulman to finish the series.

Michel originated *L'Agence Thompson and Co.* (*The Agency Thompson and Company*, 1907), while *L'Étonnante aventure de la mission Barsac* (*The Astonishing Adventure of the Barsac Mission*, 1914) was developed from his father's beginning of a novel entitled *Voyage d'études* (*Fact-Finding Mission*, 1993). *The Agency Thompson and Company* (retitled *The Thompson Travel Agency*), *The Astonishing Adventure of the Barsac Mission*, *The Survivors of the Jonathan*, *The Danube Pilot*, along with Michel's versions of his father's *The Golden Volcano* and *The Secret of Wilhelm Storitz*, had been translated for the first time by I.O. Evan in the 1960s before their true authorship was known. (Michel's *The Lighthouse at the End of the World* appeared in *The Boy's Own Paper* from 1914-1915 before book publication in 1923.)

Hence it is now possible for English-speaking readers to compare the Jules and Michel versions and judge their respective literary qualities. While there can be little question that Michel muddled a masterpiece with his changes to *The Meteor Hunt*, the elder Verne's *Magellania* read like an outline rather than a polished book in the style of *The Survivors of the Jonathan*. This same problem plagues other manuscripts that Verne completed but which neither he nor Michel saw into print, such as *Backwards to Britain* and *Paris in the 20th Century*.

Hence not only was it the altruistic efforts of several translators, but it has been the smaller, in some cases less commercial publishers, who have taken on many of the recent Verne translations, most notably the three academic presses, Oxford, Wesleyan, and Nebraska. Progress began on a third track, the plays Verne wrote, and the enthusiasm of one man who is an expert in 19th century French theater, Frank Morlock, led to his undertaking their translation, both those from the novels as well as Verne's earlier operettas and shorter works. Together, these various new translations have lifted Verne's reputation to the point where his books are now regarded as worthy of classroom treatment on America's college campuses.

The last two decades have brought astonishing progress, especially considering that the number of texts to be rendered into English has actually grown, through newly discovered manuscripts, and the unearthing of the original texts that Michel rewrote. The field has benefitted from a series of translators who have given of their skill in an effort where the intellectual reward outweighed the commercial incentive. Walter James Miller, Edward Baxter, Stanford Luce, Sidney Kravitz, William Butcher, and Frederick Paul Walter have labored mightily on behalf of Verne enthusiasts on multiple occasions, and have accomplished much against publishing standards that for many years saw Verne, not as an author of literary standing, but as simply a marquee name to be profitably strip-mined.

Still there remain a number of Verne stories that have been neglected by both commercial and academic presses. It is this gap, following the North American Jules Verne Society's precedent with *Journey Through the Impossible*, that our organization will continue to fill. Through the generosity of our late member, Edward Palik, and the pooling of expertise by a variety of Verne scholars and translators, we will be able to bring to the Anglophone public a series of hitherto unknown Verne stories.

I recall, when I first began corresponding with Ed in the 1980s, his special interest in seeing Verne translated, and how he sought to find a way to bring the overlooked Verne stories to readers. The Palik series will reflect this enthusiasm, with both short stories and novels. In addition to this volume, nearing completion is *The Count of Chanteleine*, Edward Baxter's translation of Verne's *Le Comte de Chanteleine* (1864).

The next volume will explore Michel's rewriting of his father's stories. Michel not only rewrote *Pierre-Jean* as *La Destiné de Jean Morénas* (1910, *The Fate of Jean Morénas*), but he also turned it into a 1916 feature motion picture. Both the Jules and Michel prose versions will be included. This volume will also offer *Fact-Finding Mission*, discovered since I.O. Evans translated Michel's version as *The Astonishing Adventure of the Barsac Mission*. (*The Barsac Mission* was issued in mass-market paperbacks in two parts, as *Into the Niger Bend* and *The City in the Sahara*, that remain readily available today on the second-hand market.)

Further volumes will continue to explore novels and short stories hitherto unknown to Anglophone readers, fulfilling the goal that Ed's consideration has made possible. The tales will reveal the amazing range of Verne's storytelling, in genres that may astonish those who only know his most famous stories. We hope to allow a better appreciation of the famous writer who has, for more than a century and a half, been the widest-read author of fiction in the world, and to allow him to become at last truly the best known French author in the United States.

◯

The Rehabilitation of Jules Verne In America—From Boy's Author to Adult's Author, 1960–2010

by Walter James Miller

This is really just a *progress* report on the rehabilitation of Jules Verne in America. I'm reporting mixed results, mainly luminously good news, with some residual bad news.

In most parts of the world like France, Italy, Germany, Russia, Venezuela and Taiwan, Jules Verne has always been regarded, without serious question, as a great popular writer for mature, sophisticated, intellectual adults. I'm talking about adults who are fascinated not only by Verne's scientific notions, but also by the social/political questions he raises and by the psychological and literary maneuvers he uses.

Yet in America Verne was until recently widely regarded as a children's writer, meeting only a child's intellectual needs, and few of those.

Another sinister note of suspense here (as I will show in detail later): many American publishers still profit by promoting that diminished Jules Verne as the real Jules Verne. You can check that out in your neighborhood gift shop or bookstore, or even in your average public library. To get the authentic Verne you might have to order his titles from a specialized publisher.

Notice, most American adults are puzzled when I refer to the social/political questions explored in Verne's works, or to his literary strategies. Right there is clear proof that they have not experienced the authentic Verne; the Verne the rest of the world enjoys...the Verne who could never separate science from politics or science from literary fun.

Many 20th-century parents were disturbed by this criminal situation. For instance, Willis T. Bradley, a Massachusetts academic, lamented "the free and silly adaptations made for...schoolboys nearly a hundred years ago." For his own kids, he composed several new translations, most notably *Voyage au centre de la Terre* (*Journey to the Center of the Earth*, 1864) in 1956.

True, most American adults do have fond memories of that great prophet whose books they put aside with their kiddie toys. They smile when they read that Dr. John Hunter's Quicklaunch Project at Livermore Labs, California, is experimenting with shooting payloads into space through a gun tube, and that this costs one-fortieth what it costs to lift them off by rocketry. They smile as they read a piece by a *New York Times* science reporter—or hear a KOVR-TV announcer--who calls this a replay of Verne's *De la Terre à la Lune* (*From the Earth to the Moon*, 1865). They smile again that a Jules Verne Launcher Co. in Alaska is drilling a two-mile long gun tube through a mountain. They smile knowingly when they read that scientists are generating electricity in the Caribbean by stretching cables from the warmest strata of water down to the coldest. The science reporter recalls that Captain Nemo said, offhandedly, that he could generate electricity that way if he wanted to.

Yes, most American adults do read about Jules Verne in the news. But they no longer read his books. That's kid stuff.

They're puzzled too when I talk about rehabilitating Verne. How can you rehabilitate a children's writer into an author for adults when he was a children's writer in the first place?

Why, *how*, could these criminal disparities and misunderstandings have occurred?

The easiest and simplest way for me to explain it is to tell you about my own personal part in solving this case…the case of the near-assassination of Jules Verne in America. I shall concentrate on three of Verne's works. Two of them —*From the Earth to the Moon* and *Vingt Mille Lieues sous les mers* (*Twenty Thousand Leagues Under the Sea*, 1870)—were translated into English in the 1870s. The third — *Le Superbe Orénoque* (*The Mighty Orinoco*, 1898)— was not rendered into English until 2002. It had been suppressed in English for 104 years, for political reasons, as Brian Taves has made clear in *The Jules Verne Encyclopedia* (Scarecrow Press, 1996).

Back in 1958, the Fitzroy edition was launched with I.O. Evans as editor, which ironically added to the controversy. On the one hand, Evans issued many titles Anglophone readers had never heard of. On the other, in an effort to fulfill the publisher's wish to make the books more salable to modern readers, he "decided to leave out the detail, for surely no author more repaid judicious skipping"! In addition to deleting various passages and chapters, longer Fitzroy volumes were sometimes slashed to fit the set 190 page length of a single book in the series, such as *Twenty Thousand Leagues*, *Michel Strogoff* (*Michael Strogoff*, 1876) and *L'École des Robinsons* (*The School for Robinsons*, 1882). Worse yet, Evans imposed his own political and religious attitudes on what "Verne" had said, actually regarding his own editing as "providential inspiration." So in effect he was repeating the license that the 19th century translators had arrogated to themselves.

In 1963, Simon & Schuster asked me to write an introduction to their new edition of the "standard" translation of *Twenty Thousand Leagues*. This was the 1872 version by Mercier Lewis, one of the pseudonyms of the Reverend Lewis Page Mercier, M.A. from Oxford. I came upon a strange sentence at the opening of Chapter 2, Part I. Professor Aronnax says: "I had just returned from a scientific research in the disagreeable territory of Nebraska." This so puzzled me that I resorted to the French. I found that Aronnax actually had come back from the badlands! *Badlands*…those geological phenomena of erosional sculpting and fantastically shaped hills. Now here the reader had lost a typical Verne allusion to a wonder of geography, and gained a nasty unintended and mysterious slur on Nebraska.

In the good reverend's Chapter 11, Part I, I found it strange that Captain Nemo gave no details about the batteries that powered his submarine. Checking the original for the hundredth time, I discovered that Mercier had omitted several crucial technical paragraphs. And a few pages later, he has Captain Nemo saying that his steel plates have a density of ".7 to .8 that of water." This Mercier Lewis figure is nonsensical. It would mean that Nemo's steel was lighter than water! As every high school student knows, the specific gravity of steel is 7.8.

The next great shock came when I realized that Mercier Lewis omitted a delightful scene in which Verne, the master adult educator, contrives to explain the scientific classification of fish in a very humorous fashion. So Lewis has us on a submarine journey with no details about how to propel the ship or classify the creatures outside. But science was not the only component tampered with. Lewis also disliked Nemo's politics. He left out the famous passage about Nemo's portrait gallery of heroes—like Washington, Lincoln, Kosciusko—

and of Nemo's own politically tortured family. This explains so much about Captain Nobody. He omitted Nemo's denunciation of the British treatment of the native Indian pearl divers. Isn't it strange that in our honest clergyman's "standard" translation, all reference to Darwin is eliminated?

I finally calculated that 23% of Verne's text had been junked. Lewis had omitted so much that by the time he reached the subject matter of Verne's chapter 13 he just called it chapter 12. Ironically, Verne's chapter 13, "The Nautilus," is missing entirely from Lewis' table of contents!

Of course, these cuts meant that not only Verne's scientific and philosophical, but also his literary integrity had been destroyed. The "standard" translation features a haphazard story line, shallow characterization, and an intellectual depth of near zero. We have been stuck with this version for five generations. At least five publishing houses still issue this version as authentic Verne. Other translators working in the 1870s and 1880s were equally unreliable and even tendentious in their renderings. For example, W.H.G. Kingston, in translating *L'Île mystérieuse* (*The Mysterious Island*, 1875), actually rewrote Captain Nemo's deathbed speech to make it less critical of British imperialism. The one novel to escape such cynical treatment was *Le Tour du monde en quatre-vingts jours* (*Around the World in Eighty Days*, 1872). How come? By then Verne had become so famous that as each chapter of this work appeared in a French magazine serialization, foreign correspondents cabled home a summary! Naturally, when the translator came to that novel, he could leave nothing out!

Indeed, I soon found that a Philadelphia teacher had, as early as 1874, complained that an American version of *Cinq Semaines en ballon* (*Five Weeks in a Balloon*, 1863) "contains so many geographical mistakes that it must have been done in a hurry." He wrote that "hasty translations of Verne's later works by English hands," with "some of the best passages omitted," were being sold in America. The intrinsic value, the uniqueness of Verne's work still managed to shine through. Our Broad Street Academy teacher went on to say that "these translations… spread like wildfire…and were everywhere hailed with the greatest delight by young and old."

There's a tragicomic ending to this tale of the Philadelphia teacher, named Edward Roth. He himself got caught up in the frenzy. He put out a now infamous American version of *From the Earth to the Moon* and *Autour de la Lune* (*Around the Moon*, 1869) in which he has Verne write a poem about the City of Brotherly Love, talk in the first person, and invent many pro-American episodes that even the America-lover Verne could never have dared. Roth so heavily re-wrote Verne that he shamelessly bragged in his introduction that he "improved" on the Great Romancer! A tragic precedent had been renewed: knowing no better, people would buy any incomplete and ersatz Verne book.

Needless to say, literary critics in America and other Anglophone countries, reading Verne only in the English editions, considered him a very poor writer. They considered his work fit only for children. The low point in American attitudes toward Verne came in 1961, when *Galaxy* magazine published an article that sneered at Verne for creating steel so light that sheets of it would float, and for failing to give the specs for his batteries. Of course, the author, T.L. Thomas, like all other American critics, blamed Verne himself instead of his translators. Even such a science fiction intellectual as Damon Knight was taken in. Verne's reputation in America was destroyed.

My editor at Simon & Schuster agreed that we could not help perpetuate Mercier Lewis' travesty. He assigned me to do a new translation. While I was working on it, I discovered another horrible trend in Verne publishing in English. Anthony Bonner had put out, in 1962, a version of *Twenty Thousand Leagues* that was 99% complete in content but had new flaws. When in doubt about what Verne meant Bonner relied on the Mercier Lewis edition; for example, on Nemo's steel being .7 to .8 the density of water! And although, while consulting Lewis, Bonner must certainly have discovered Lewis' crimes, he said nothing about them in his introduction, because he wrote no introduction. He neither exposed Lewis nor claimed a first for himself. And Bonner's own mistake in following Lewis remained uncorrected for four decades until Frederick Paul Walter helped Bantam put out a new edition in 2003.

So now there are two Lewis legacies to contend with. Some publishers still issue the Mercier Lewis translations intact, as in 1872; and others correct his more obvious mistakes but do not restore the passages he cut.

The most valuable feature of my Simon & Schuster translation, which appeared in 1965, was that I did write an introduction—"Jules Verne in America"—which did what Bonner could have done. Simon & Schuster had to rush out a second printing before publication because the first was snatched up by a book club! I was invited to explain my edition on twenty-seven radio and TV shows in just the first month! The *Reader's Digest Best Loved Books* series bought the rights to produce a condensed version. Yes, the irony of it: my version, done largely to close the gaps in the "standard" translation, was now issued in a popular new condensation, with gaps all its own.

It would be four decades before I got the full story. Norman Wolcott, a fellow member in the North American Jules Verne Society, delivered a paper that was a brilliant piece of detective work. It explains why the clergyman was reduced to doing rush hack translations, how he actually and helplessly made most of the hundreds of errors that are still enshrined in his editions.

But at least the rehabilitation movement was underway, among scholars and the more enlightened science fiction fans. A year or so later my Simon & Schuster editor moved to the New American Library and of course he wanted a New American Library edition of *Twenty Thousand Leagues*. Across the hall from my office at New York University sat a distinguished Romance language teacher, Mendor Thomas Brunetti. I talked him into doing the New American Library translation, and that gave me a chance to get into print some important improvements over my Simon & Schuster edition. And in 2001, when New American Library decided to put out a new edition of Brunetti's book, I got to write an afterword in which I put into the record for the first time the story of our collaboration.

Later Brian Taves told me that these early Miller-Brunetti efforts inspired him to become a Verne scholar. Now Verne became respectable in the academic world.

In 1953, the very first doctoral dissertation on Verne had been completed – not by a European, but an American, Stanford L. Luce, Jr. at Yale. Several decades later, when Arthur Evans and William Butcher also wrote their dissertations on the Great Romancer, Luce emerged as a Verne translator, as did Butcher.

For a while it looked as if the anti-Lewis forces had won a major victory. But no. Most commercial publishers continued to put out expensive, handsome, beautifully illustrated gift editions of Mercier Lewis. In the 1970s there were fifteen such editions, many of them not identified as Mercier Lewis' work, but all of them featuring that disagreeable territory of Nebraska!

So by 1974 we Verne lovers sank back down in the depths of despair. Verne was still in trouble in America. Then one of the great editors of our time, Hugh Rawson at the famous old T.Y. Crowell Co., had an idea. He reminded me of the fabulous success of *The Annotated Alice* by Martin Gardner. Why not make our case through annotated editions? We could annotate Mercier Lewis' three-quarters of *Twenty Thousand Leagues* to show his errors, and add [in brackets] my new version of the remaining quarter that Lewis had omitted, to show the damage he had done to Verne's reputation.

In 1976 T.Y. Crowell published the first volume of *The Annotated Jules Verne*. My afterword was optimistically titled "Jules Verne Rehabilitated." The jacket was graced with blurbs by such luminaries as Isaac Asimov and Kurt Vonnegut. Asimov pictured Verne as "surely.... smiling from his grave," because "for the first time [*Twenty Thousand Leagues Under the Sea*] appears in English as it was in French, together with fascinating notes that place it in the context of its time." And Vonnegut imagined that "Few science-fiction stories could match [the editor's] adventures in resurrecting a great author, Jules Verne, in love and scholarship."

Crowell ran a three-column ad in *The New York Times Book Review*. The famous journalist Herbert Mitgang wrote a news article about this expose! The young German Volker Dehs, now an illustrious Verne scholar, bought a copy of it while he was in America and has praised it ever since. The French critics noted that this was the first annotated edition of Verne anywhere. And it became a Book-of-the-Month Club Book Dividend! Now, I felt, we've really rehabilitated the Great Romancer in the Anglophone world.

So in 1978 Crowell published the second volume, a complete new translation of *From the Earth to the Moon*, with annotations and appendices to show the errors and distortions in the 19th century versions by Mercier Lewis and Edward Roth. I demonstrated that, properly and completely rendered, this genuine space novel was also an anti-war classic on a level with Aristophanes' *Lysistrata* and Joseph Heller's *Catch-22*. I showed how Lewis once again had diluted Verne's anti-imperialism and emasculated his anti-militarism. But before my edition was published, T.Y. Crowell was absorbed by HarperCollins, who had no further interest in annotated science fiction except to sell subsidiary rights. For example, a Japanese publisher bought the rights to translate my edition wholesale.

It has come out twice in a neat two-volume paperback format. Even my name Miller was rendered into ideograms. However, in 1995 Gramercy put out an updated edition of my original, annotated translation.

Rehabilitation seemed now safely in progress, but Mercier Lewis and Edward Roth and W.H.G. Kingston versions were still mainstay Verne in gift shops, book stores, libraries.

And then I faced a comical dilemma. Scribner's asked me to write chapter 75, about Jules Verne, in a massive tome to be called *Writers for Children*. If I declined because I don't see him as primarily a writer for children, somebody else would write him up as exactly that. So I somehow diplomatically made the case that Verne wrote for all ages, that as a matter of fact in France he is issued mainly in adult editions but also in special children's editions, but properly translated, he is an author for adults even in English.

Then came a big surprise, a major victory! United States Naval Institute Press asked Brian Taves at the Library of Congress to nominate someone to do a special deluxe annotated translation of *Twenty Thousand Leagues*. After I was one-third through I got the bright idea to take aboard Frederick Paul Walter, whose translation for Random House had run afoul of anti-Verne prejudice. I especially wanted Rick as a collaborator because he is well-versed in marine biology and technology and has done exhaustive research on the proper American names for the thousands of species of fish that Verne describes. Naval Institute Press produced our edition in 1993 and our editor there claims that it's their longest title still in print; it's now in its fourth printing.

Soon after, when Butcher produced a mass paperback edition through Oxford University Press, he made us feel good because he quoted us twenty-two times. Readers of English now have both quality and mass paperback editions, thoroughly annotated from the historical, biographical, technical, and literary points of view.

Brian Taves summed up our work in the Summer 1999 issue of *Extrapolation*: "Walter James Miller," he wrote, "first vividly exposed the drawbacks of earlier Verne translations in the preface to his 1965 edition. Miller elaborated on these problems in his Annotated Verne Series and other scholars have since followed his lead."

For example, Wesleyan University Press has launched its Early Classics of Science Fiction Series, with a team of Verne scholars including Arthur Evans, Sidney Kravitz, Stanford Luce, William

Butcher, and me, following my own lead. Thus in 2002 Wesleyan issued Luce's first-ever English translation of *The Mighty Orinoco*, originally suppressed in English for political reasons. This well-plotted novel, as I show in my Introduction and Notes, is strongly anti-colonialist and pro-feminist, even androgynist. It is well-reviewed on Amazon.com. And a year later, the North American Jules Verne Society issued Verne's science fiction play, *Voyage à travers l'impossible* (*Journey Through the Impossible*, 1882), in a handsome volume published by Prometheus Books.

Many other English editions of Verne for adult audiences followed. In 2006, to mention just one, the University of Nebraska Press issued Verne's own original version of *La Chasse au météore* (*The Meteor Hunt*, 1908), translated and annotated by Frederick Paul Walter and Walter James Miller.

But as I warned you, there is still residual bad news. The worst shock came in perusing the 2005 Barnes & Noble edition of five novels in one fat book. *It shows that now we have made some publishers well aware of the Mercier Lewis problem but they have found a new, unethical way around it*. The title page credits the translation to the good reverend, with introduction and notes by Victoria Lake. She lets mistakes like "the disagreeable territory" go by without comment. When she comes to a major omission, like Verne's "long passage in which Conseil lectures Ned on the scientific classification of fish," she does acknowledge the literary value of the scene—but still omits it!

The Quality Paperback Book Club, Scholastic Magazine Press, Wordsworth Press, and Nelson/Doubleday all still issue the Mercier Lewis as genuine Verne. Will we ever be able to stamp out Mercier Lewis if Scholastic proffers him to public school children in an edition cut by *another* third? If Wordsworth feeds Lewis's Verne to college students; Nelson/Doubleday to its Science Fiction Book Club members; and Barnes & Noble and QPBC to adults everywhere? And Tor, a science-fiction specialty publisher, who must surely know better, continues to blithely offer Lewis to the unsuspecting science fiction reader? So too Kingston's propagandized *Mysterious Island* is still on the shelves of leading chain bookstores.

Lewis is not alone; Roth lives too. In 2009 Dover reprinted again their 1960 edition of the wretched 1874 Roth translation of *From the Earth to the Moon*. Miller and Taves warned Dover about Roth, and that if necessary to use a public domain translation, better ones were available. Hence Dover acted "with malice aforethought;" they were hardly ignorant of the literary crime.

Thanks to publishers like these, many American adults still do not know the genuine prophet of science fiction; do not know about his social and political stance or his splendid literary talents.

Jules Verne foresaw not only the environmental crisis, the endangered species crisis; the possibility of crossing the Poles by sailing under them; of producing self-renewing energy by inexpensively running cables down through several strata of sea; of establishing underwater towns, mines, farms, and labs; of escaping gravity by using gun-tubes instead of rocketry.

He also foresaw the collapse of colonialism, the emergence of new attitudes about gender, the industrialization of China, the smoldering of French separatism in Canada, the rise of the American Goliath, the prostitution of science by new power elites: by private financiers and the military-industrial complex. Thanks to Scholastic and Barnes & Noble and others of this stripe, American children and adults hardly know this side of Verne. They hardly know the Verne who explored all varieties of nonconformism, from vagabondism to guerrilla war to philosophical anarchism; the Verne who gave a voice in his books to every shade of social and political opinion, from utopian socialism to anti-semitism to proto-fascism. Indeed, the great French scholar Jean Chesneaux ranks Jules Verne with H.G. Wells as a major writer of political fiction.

Why are so few *commercial* publishers interested in the authentic Jules Verne?

Well, Mercier Lewis, W.H.G. Kingston, and Edward Roth are in the public domain: they no longer have to be paid for their work. And these publishers by now have a heavy investment in their children's-level illustrations. And the children's-level editions are 'non-controversial': they are fumigated of anti-colonialism, anti-imperialism, anti-militarism, and pro-feminism!

But the tide is being reversed. Americans now have some access to the Jules Verne who can create three-dimensional characters; who can accent some characters as archetypes; who can create mood and atmosphere, convincing motivation, authentic dream states, and wonderment and respect for Nature; who is mature and responsible in seeing science and technology as intertwined with social-political conditions.

American readers can now have the authentic Verne that sea captains in Murmansk, bank tellers in Caracas, and mathematicians in Paris have always enjoyed. The Verne who has been a perennial challenge to literary critics in Europe is now a growing challenge to scholars and critics in the U.S.A. But to get that real Verne you might have to be sure you get an authentic version!

○

The North American Jules Verne Society has issued for sale a CD with four of the radio shows that Walter mentions; see the society's website, www.najvs.org, for details.

Jules Verne's Humor:
A Portfolio of Original French Engravings

Verne's talent for comedy, exemplified in this volume, has been unjustly overlooked, and can be found throughout his oeuvre. It was first evidenced in his early theatrical background and combined with adventure in his novels *Le Tour du Monde en quatre-vingt jours* (*Around the World in Eighty Days*, 1873), *Les Tribulations de un Chinois en Chine* (*The Tribulations of a Chinese in China*, 1879), *L'Ecole des Robinsons* (*The School for Robinsons*, 1882), *Kéraban-le-têtu* (*Keraban the Inflexible*, 1883), *Clovis Dardentor* (1896), and *Le Testament d'un Excentrique* (*The Will of an Eccentric*, 1899). Verne's humor often has its basis in bizarre characters, many of them placed in unusual locales, such as Kin-Fo in China, Keraban in Turkey, Phileas Fogg in virtually any corner of the world, or the American who formulates a truly living *Will of an Eccentric*. *Clovis Dardentor* is a farce of familial and inheritance complications against a background of travel, which Verne dedicated to his three grandsons. *The School for Robinsons* satirizes the Robinsonade narrative of survival on a desert island.

"Le Humbug" ("The Humbug," 1910) and *Aventures de la famille Raton* (*Adventures of the Rat Family*, 1891) are lighthearted treatments of Darwinism. In the former, a P.T. Barnum-type huckster claims to have discovered bones of a giant prehistoric man in New York state, while the latter is a fairy tale of a family climbing the evolutionary ladder in a succession of incarnations. A similar theme, this time used to mock colonialism, is found in "Gil Braltar" (1887), wherein a general is so hirsute that he is able to lead an army of gorillas in defense of the British stronghold. In the same spirit, "Monsieur Ré-Dièze et

Mademoiselle Mi-Bémol" ("Mr. Ray Sharp and Miss Me Flat," 1893), portrays children's voices substituting for the musical intonations of a cathedral organ.

In *Un Fantaisie du Docteur Ox* (*A Fancy of Doctor Ox*, 1872), Verne cleverly mocks his own literary formula, with the mad escapade of a scientist who fills a small town's atmosphere with oxygen, speeding up the pace of living to a frenzy. *Sans dessus dessous* (*Topsy Turvy*, 1889) burlesques Verne's own heroes from *De la Terre à la lune* and its sequel *Autour de la lune* (*From the Earth to the Moon* and *Around the Moon*, 1865 and 1870, respectively) by exposing their greed as they ruthlessly plan to shift the world's axis for their own enrichment, heedless of the cost to life, instead earning ridicule when their calculations go awry and nothing happens. Science is again parodied in *La Chasse au météore* (*The Meteor Hunt*, 1908), in which two Americans begin a Hatfield/McCoy-style feud over precedence in discovering a meteor, which becomes echoed in international rivalry when it is discovered to be made of gold and hurtling toward the Earth. Michel Verne authored "Au XXIXᵉ siècle: Journée d'un journaliste américain en 2889" ("In the Twenty-Ninth Century: The Day of an American Journalist in 2889," 1889), originally published under his father's name, and which his father proudly rewrote, a look at what the future a millennia hence and how much life may remain the same.

Verne subjects Ox and many of the heroes of his more serious novels to a farcical humiliation in *Voyage à travers l'Impossible* (*Journey Through the Impossible*, 1882), one of the plays he coauthored with Adolphe d'Ennery. Other plays more directly inspired by his books, *Around the World in Eighty Days* (1874) and *Keraban the Inflexible* (1883), revel in the amusement offered by their sources.

The Marriage of Mr. Anselme des Tilleuls and *Jédédias Jamet, or The Tale of an Inheritance* are not the only humorous stories of Verne to newly appear in English. While the classic *Around the World in Eighty Days* along with *The Tribulations of a Chinese in China*, *The School for Robinsons*, *Keraban the Inflexible*, *Clovis Dardentor*, and *The Will of an Eccentric* were translated shortly after their original appearance, even the latter two just recently appeared in the United States after initial publication only in Britain. *Around the World in Eighty Days* and *A Fancy of Dr. Ox* have received modern translation, and in 2006 Jules's original version of *The Meteor Hunt* appeared for the first time, nearly a century after Michel's revision had been translated as *The Chase of the Golden Meteor*. They have joined the first ever English appearances in the 1990s of *Adventures of the Rat Family* and "The Humbug." Some of the plays, too, are recent discoveries, including *Journey Across the Impossible* in 1981, *Keraban the Inflexible* in 1989, and in 2004 the first playscript of *Around the World in Eighty Days*, actually written before the novel.

The following pages offer a range of original engravings, frontispieces, and covers from these stories and plays, embodying their themes.

◯

1872, A Fancy of Dr. Ox.

1873, *Around the World in Eighty Days* (novel).

1874, *Around the World in Eighty Days* (play)

1879, *The Tribulations of a Chinese in China.*

1882, *Journey Through the Impossible.*

1882, *The School for Robinsons*.

1883, *Keraban the Inflexible* (novel).

1883, *Keraban the Inflexible* (play).

1887, *Gil Braltar.*

1889, *In the Twenty-Ninth Century--The Day of an American Journalist in 2889.*

1889, *Topsy Turvy.*

1891, *Adventures of the Rat Family.*

1893, *Mr. Ray Sharp and Miss Me Flat.*

1896, *Cloviis Dardentor.*

1899, *The Will of an Eccentric.*

1908, *The Meteor Hunt*.

1910, *The Humbug.*

Preface:

The Marriage of
Mr. Anselme des Tilleuls

by Jean-Michel Margot

In 1858, Jules Verne was 30 years old. The previous year, on January 10, he had married Honorine Deviane, a widow with two young daughters. The household lived at 18 Boulevard Poissonnière in Paris. To make a living, Jules worked as a stockbroker at 72 Rue de Provence.

The not-yet-known novelist had already published short stories, plays, and operettas.[1] His *Un Voyage en ballon* (*Voyage in a Balloon*, 1851) had even been translated in America.[2] His literary fame, however—that of the "Voyages Extraordinaires" ("Extraordinary Journeys"), inaugurated with the publication of *Cinq semaines en ballon* (*Five Weeks in a Balloon*, 1863)—was still a few years in the future.[3]

Not everything written by the novelist-to-be has been published, even in French and even today, in 2009. In 1995, *Le Mariage de M. Anselme des Tilleuls* (*The Marriage of Mr. Anselme des Tilleuls*) was among the almost-unknown manuscripts.

In 1991, this short story was published for the first time in Switzerland.[4] Two years later, it was available in France with two

---

1. The most complete and up-to-date bibliography of works by Jules Verne can be found at http://jv.gilead.org.il/biblio/ .

2. Jules Verne, "Voyage in a Balloon," *Sartain's Union Magazine of Literature and Art* (May 1852), 389-395.

3. Christian Robin, *Un Monde connu et inconnu: Jules Verne* (Nantes: Centre universitaire de recherches verniennes, 1978), 288.

4. Jules Verne, *Le Mariage de M. Anselme des Tilleuls* (Porrentruy: L'Olifant, 1991), 132. Preface by Michel Tournier, postface by Jean-Michel Margot. Jules Verne

other Vernian short stories.[5] These two editions were used to translate the story and to write this preface, which is, in great part, what was published in Switzerland in 1991.

When Verne wrote *The Marriage* is not certain, with Olivier Dumas suggesting 1855 and Daniel Compère two or three years later. The manuscript was signed by Jules Verne, but not dated.

The other two short stories published in 1991 with *The Marriage*— *San Carlos* (*San Carlos*) and *Le Siège de Rome* (*The Siege of Rome*)— had been written in the mid-1850s.[6] Verne, whom we know today as the "politically correct" writer for the French bourgeoisie, wrote many stories, poems, and plays that could have been considered as marginal, or even offensive, in the middle of the 19th century. Considered by Daniel Compère to be the best Verne "vaudeville" (light comedy), *The Marriage of Mr. Anselme des Tilleuls* is a good example of such light, hilarious, and sarcastic literature.[7]

The manuscript remained in the Verne family until July 8, 1981, when the city of Nantes (Verne's birthplace) purchased the manuscripts after the death of Jean Jules-Verne, grandson of the writer.

In 1935, two Jules Verne fans, Jean Guermonprez and Cornelis Helling, founded the Société Jules Verne. The first issue of the Société's *Bulletin*, under the pen of Cornelis Helling, mentions *The Marriage of Mr. Anselme des Tilleuls* for the first time in the history of Vernian studies. [8] And with the first mention of this title appears the first mistake: Instead of *des Tilleuls*, Helling writes *Du Tilleul*.

The Société Jules Verne did not survive World War II, but it was brought back to life in the late 1960s. The title of the short story was correctly spelled in the first issue of the new series of the *Bulletin*, but a

wrote "Mr." on the title page of his manuscript. This original edition has a modern correct "M." in the title.

5. Jules Verne, *San Carlos et autres récits inédits* (Paris: le cherche-midi éditeur, 1993), 288. Comments and notes about *Le Mariage de Mr. Anselme des Tilleuls* by Claudine Sainlot and Christian Robin.

6. Both short stories were published in the above-mentioned volume (see Note 5).

7. Daniel Compère, "A la recherche des systèmes nouveaux," *Bulletin de la Société Jules Verne*, no 63 (1982), 250-258.

8. Cornelis Helling, "L'oeuvre de Jules Verne," *Bulletin de la Société Jules Verne*, no 1 (November 1935), 15-21.

Jules Verne in 1850, age 22

second mistake was introduced: The work was now classified as a play.[9] No date for the text was mentioned.

Charles-Noël Martin, in his 1971 bio-bibliography, did not add

9. Olivier Dumas, Joseph Laissus, and Louis Le Garsmeur, "Bibliographie des oeuvres de Jules Verne," *Bulletin de la Société Jules Verne*, no 1 (1967), 7-12.

Le Marquis Anselme des Tilleuls avait, en 1842, atteint l'âge non moins raisonnable que pubère de 27 ans. C'est l'époque ultramontaine de l'existence à laquelle les ~~jeunes hommes~~ adolescents ou jouissent avec les folies d'une jeunesse utilisée, à moins qu'ils ne les commencent heureuse ~~période~~ de la vie, où l'on peut faire ce qui, dans une langue énergique et paternelle, s'appelle des bêtises !

Bref, Anselme des Tilleuls représentait un ~~jeune adolescent~~ jeune homme blond, tirant sur les couchers de soleil ; ses cheveux en rébellion ouverte avec les lois de la géométrie capillo-pratique, proposaient aux coiffeurs es-sciences un ~~problème~~ théorème insoluble, dont les corollaires hardis et hérissés jetaient la terreur parmi ses fillettes à la ronde : mais en revanche, des bras Ouistititiens, des jambes jouant l'échasse, des yeux irréconciliables, une bouche meublée en palissandre, des oreilles d'école primaire, prêtaient au jeune marquis un charme inexprimé, un attrait inexprimable.

Grand de corps et petit d'idées, large de poitrine, mais étroit de cerveau, fort des épaules, mais faible d'esprit, riche de charpente, et pauvre d'intelligence ; soit en amoncelant des montagnes comme Encelade, soit en vivant d'une existence purement végétale, il devait à coup sûr gagner le royaume des Cieux !

Cependant Anselme des Tilleuls jouissait d'un succès d'estime, quand on l'envisageait d'assez loin ; comme les hauts monuments, il ~~voulait~~ se la de l'éloignant d'une perspective réhabilitante ; à cent pas de distance, on eut dit d'une architecture pyramidale,

The first page of the manuscript of *The Marriage of Mr. Anselme des Tilleuls.*

The last page of the manuscript of *The Marriage of Mr. Anselme des Tilleuls.*

anything new, wrote the title correctly, but put it among the plays.[10] André Bottin, in his 1978 bibliography, lists *The Marriage of Mr. Anselme des Tilleuls* again as a play and without a date.[11]

The first to describe the short story correctly was Daniel Compère in 1978, in a bibliography overlooked completely by Vernian scholars.[12] The first to study and report on *The Marriage of Mr. Anselme des Tilleuls* was Charles-Noël Martin in his Ph.D. dissertation of 1980, which offered a portrayal of the Marquis des Tilleuls.[13]

The purchase of the Vernian manuscripts by the city of Nantes allowed many researchers and specialists to see and read the text of *The Marriage of Mr. Anselme des Tilleuls.* In 1984, Daniel Compère and Olivier Dumas studied the short story and published their comments, followed by Piero Gondolo della Riva in 1985, who listed *Le Marriage* among the never-published short stories.[14]

---

10. Charles-Noël Martin, *Jules Verne, sa vie et son oeuvre* (Lausanne: Rencontre, 1971), 350.

11. André Bottin, *Bibliographie des éditions illustrées des Voyages extraordinaires de Jules Verne en cartonnage d'éditeur de la collection Hetzel* (Conte: chez l'auteur, 1978), 568.

12. Daniel Compère, *Bibliographie des oeuvres de Jules Verne* (Amiens: Centre de documentation Jules Verne, 1978), 5.

13. Charles-Noël Martin, *Recherche sur la nature, les origines et le traitement de la science dans l'oeuvre de Jules Verne* (Paris: Sorbonne - Université Paris 7, 1980), 618.

14. Olivier Dumas, "Le Mariage de Mr. Anselme des Tilleuls, nouvelle inattendue," *Bulletin de la Société Jules Verne*, no 63 (1982), 259-264; Olivier Dumas, "Bibliograpie des nouvelles, articles, discours et récits de Jules Verne," *Bulletin*

By then, the short story was well known among the small and close circle of Jules Verne specialists, but it needed to become available to a larger audience of readers. This was accomplished in French in 1991. It now appears in English with this first edition, allowing the Anglophone reader to savor an unknown Jules Verne who uses a brilliant "how-to-write" talent and a humor prominent in the later novels.

The young Marquis Anselme des Tilleuls, at 27 still a virgin, is an idiotic and dreadful descendant of an ancient noble family. One of his ancestors had been ennobled in 879 by King Louis the Stammerer (846-879), after using the leaves of a linden tree to purge the royal visitor of a digestive blockage. Anselme's pious tutor Paraclet tries to find him a wife. With time passing, Paraclet must gradually scale down his wishes—source of many comic scenes—finally choosing a clerk's middle-aged daughter who is overweight beyond imagination.

Beyond the ironical, even farcical, nature of this short story in which the author uses with ease the ribald metaphor, and plays with words and scatological meaning, we can identify two main interests. The first one is the subject of the story, marriage. In the mid-1850s, marriage is for Jules Verne, although he denies it, a major concern. His mother, living in Nantes, wants her son, then living in Paris, to marry, and in several letters he told her that the ill-fated love of his younger years had prevented him from marital ties. Every marriage is an object of derision and so is the marriage of Anselme des Tilleuls.

In 1855 Verne was twenty-seven, the same age as his hero (or antihero) when he wrote this caprice. The second important aspect of the short story is the role played in the narration by grammar and Latin literature.

The subtitle of the short story reveals Verne's purpose: *Souvenirs d'un élève de huitième* (*Memories of an Eighth-Grader*). Verne settles old scores with his former high-school teachers and the provincial aristocracy of his birthplace. The town of C…is Nantes, and tutor Naso Paraclet, senior Latinist and disciple of Lhomond, represents a teacher at Saint-Stanislas, the Nantes boarding school where the young Jules Verne studied for a

de la Société Jules Verne, no 63 (1982), 278-282 ; Daniel Compère, "Les inédits de Jules Verne," *Bulletin de la Société Jules Verne*, no 64 (1982), 290-291; Piero Gondolo della Riva, *Bibliographie analytique de toutes les oeuvres de Jules Verne. Volume II: oeuvres romanesques publiées et oeuvres inédites* (Paris: Société Jules Verne, 1985) 160.

few years, including 1842, when Anselme des Tilleuls celebrates his 27th year, according to the first sentence of the story.

Research in Nantes could probably reveal the identity of the Latinist targeted by Verne. The Latin language constitutes one of the main engines of the story, and the memories of the declensions and conjugations that he needed to memorize were still resonating in the writer's spirit, many years after the end of his studies.

For more than 200 years, the pillar of all Latin studies in France has consisted of two works by Lhomond, whose grammatical examples have crossed time to continue their use in schools today. The abbot Charles-François Lhomond was born in Chaulnes (Picardy) in 1727. He was regent of sixth grade in the Collège of Cardinal-Lemoine, and professor emeritus of the University of Paris. He died on December 31, 1794. Lhomond is characterized by a passion for teaching Latin. He wrote a number of Latin works, which were then translated into French, English, or Spanish. Today, Latin students still use his *De Viris illustribus urbis Romae, a Romulo ad Augustum* (*Life of the famous men of Rome, from Romulus to Augustus*), a work based on the writings of Plutarch and characterized by the fact that this same text is used to inculcate in beginner, average, and advanced students the rules of Latin grammar. The other work to which Jules Verne refers is *Eléments de grammaire latine* (1779), which, thanks to its clearness and happy choice of examples, was reprinted in dozens of editions in France during the 19th century, each professor adding his own variations, comments, and explanations. Because every student needed his (or her) own copy, the sum of all these various editions makes the *Lhomond Grammar* the best-selling book of all time. To write *The Marriage of Mr. Anselme des Tilleuls*, Verne used an 1800 edition, *Elémens (sic) de la grammaire latine par Lhomond, professeur émérite en la ci-devant Université de Paris* (*Elements of Latin grammar by Lhomond, professor emeritus at the University of Paris*). This twelfth edition was published in Paris by Colas, Bookseller, in the eighth year of the "République françoise (sic) une et indivisible" (French Republic, one and indivisible). The work has XII and 288 pages, and was published just after the French Revolution, under the Directoire.

The tone of Verne's short story intends to scoff and mock, with wordplay and ridiculous use of proper names alternating with the Latinisms of the schoolboy. The examples (drawn from Lhomond) and the quotations of Virgil make it possible for the young author to trace throughout his account a grammatical comparison between marriage and the Latin conjugations.

The character of the tutor, bearing the name of Naso Paraclet, heralds all the ridiculous scientists of the novels to come, such as Paganel in *Les Enfants du capitaine Grant* (*The Children of Captain Grant*, 1867) and Benedict in *Un Capitaine de quinze ans* (*A Captain at Fifteen*, 1878) (as depicted in an engraving in the original French edition on the opposite page). Similarly, Paraclet forms with his pupil Anselme a father-and-son couple that foreshadows the other couples to appear in the still-to-be-written "Extraordinary Journeys." As in the later novels, the proper names of the characters in the short story indicate the characters' roles in the narration.

Not only is the Latin language one of the guides through *The Marriage of Mr. Anselme des Tilleuls*, it is also used by Verne to create the proper names of his characters. Madame de Mirabelle (from *mirare*, to admire, and *bellus*, beautiful), President Pertinax (from *per*, end to end, and *tenere*, to hold; thus obstinate and stubborn), and Maro Lafourchette (reference to Virgil, whose complete Latin name is Publius Vergilius Maro)—all of these names are transparent, requiring no transformation to detect their secret meaning.[15] Naso Paraclet (a reference to Ovid, whose complete Latin name is Publius Ovidius Naso) deserves a particular mention, because *Paraclet* is also another name for the Holy Spirit in French.[16] Verne undoubtedly wanted such a name in opposition to the

---

15. Virgil, Latin poet (70 - 19 B.C.), author of the *Eclogues*, ten pastoral poems; the *Georgics*, a poem on agriculture in four books; and the *Aeneid*, a national epic in twelve books.

   Marie Belloc, better known as a writer under the name Mrs. Belloc-Lowndes, paid a visit to Jules Verne ten years before his death. In the report she wrote in *The Strand Magazine* (February 1895), pp. 206-213, she quotes Virgil among the authors appearing in the library of Jules Verne and among the "very worn books."

16. Ovid, Latin poet (43 - 17 B.C.) and author of the *Metamorphoses*, fifteen books in hexameter, an encyclopedia of myths from the creation of the world to the apotheosis of Caesar.

   Paraclete comes from the Greek word παράκλητος (paráklētos, "one who consoles, one who intercedes on our behalf, a comforter or an advocate"). Paraclete appears in the New Testament in the Gospel of John, where it may be translated into English as "counselor," "helper," or "comforter." The early church identified the Paraclete as the Holy Spirit, and Christians continue to use Paraclete as a title for the Spirit of God.

pious family circle and perhaps even against the religious bigots among whom he had been reared. The first name of Naso also lets us imagine a nasal appendage of unusual dimensions with which Verne wished to decorate the face of the Marquis's professor. A few years before, on December 31, 1852, Verne wrote his mother a letter (categorized by Olivier Dumas as a "picturesque one") that began as follows— "Madame, I have just learned from the lips of your son, that you had the intention to send him some handkerchiefs"—and that ended with: "I am, Madame, with new handkerchiefs, the

Benedict in *A Fifteen-Year-Old Captain.*

very respectful nose of Mister your son. Nabuco, for amplification, Jules Verne."[17] In that letter the young playwright, who still had to wait more than ten years before becoming a well-known novelist, described his nose thoroughly to obtain handkerchiefs from his mother.

The tone of this letter and its object obviously bring it close to *The Marriage of Mr. Anselme des Tilleuls*, whose name has in French a sufficient sonority to make it already surprising and hilarious.

The manuscript, as noted by Daniel Compère, remained in the state of a draft close to its final version. Reading shows that it is indeed a copy (there are a few corrections), but as the author was progressing in his copying, he discovered grammatical mistakes, repetitions, spelling errors, or just a better way to write an expression or a sentence.[18] For example,

---

17. Letter by Jules Verne to his mother, December 31, 1852 (Vaulon collection), published by Olivier Dumas in the *Bulletin de la Société Jules Verne*, 1982, vol. 17, no. 83, pp. 8-9. This letter had previously been mentioned by Jean Jules-Verne and Marc Soriano.

18. The first and last pages of the manuscript are available online at http://www. arkhenum.fr/bm_nantes/jules_verne/_app_php_mysql/ms/recherche_alpha_

Jules Verne wrote in the manuscript the name of the grammarian Lhomond with an apostrophe (L'Homond) before discovering that the apostrophe was a mistake. For this publication, the correct spelling and punctuation were restored.

Between 1855 and 1860, Jules Verne mastered his style, both at the level of knowledge expressed by a rich, selective vocabulary, and at the level of know-how expressed by the construction of the entire text, which makes its reading pleasant and consistent. Daniel Compère quotes three passages of *The Marriage of Mr. Anselme des Tilleuls* showing how well Jules Verne controls the fields of mathematical, geographical, and military vocabulary.

The Marriage of Mr. Anselme des Tilleuls is an itinerary in three wedding steps before reaching its goal—the marriage of the hero—that combines an epic with bawdy innuendo, with the whole being supported by the comical use of the Latin language.

The annotations include translations and explanations that help readers enjoy this aspect of Vernian humor. *The Marriage of Mr. Anselme des Tilleuls* is one of the last texts written by Jules Verne before his discovery of Edgar Allan Poe.

Poe was an independent source of literary inspiration for Verne. Baudelaire began translating Poe as early as 1848, and in 1856, and this work was published as *Histoires extraordinaires* (*The Extraordinary Stories*), followed in 1857 by *Nouvelles histoires extraordinaires* (*The New Extraordinary Stories*). The American author allowed the French novelist to improve his literary style, allowing him to create imaginary and utopian universes that were nonetheless based on the knowledge and science of his time.

◯

---

cles.php?titre=anselme. The whole manuscript has 30 pages and is available online, but only for people who are conducting research on the manuscripts and must see them. The site is www.bm.nantes.fr; click on *Collections numérisées*. The reader is asked to complete a short questionnaire, because the Municipal Library of Nantes wants to know the object of the reader's studies and research. And, of course, it's available only in French!

The Marriage of
Mr. Anselme des Tilleuls

by Jules Verne

Translated by Edward Baxter

In 1842 the Marquis Anselme des Tilleuls had attained the rational and pubescent age of twenty-seven years. This is the ultramontane period of existence, when adolescents put away the follies of their spent youth (unless, perhaps, they are just embarking on them), a happy time of life, when it is permissible to commit what are referred to, in forceful, paternal language, as stupidities.

Anselme des Tilleuls may be described briefly as a young man with a fair, almost sunset-colored complexion. His hair, in open rebellion against the laws of practical capillary geometry, presented the most highly-skilled hairdressers with an insoluble theorem, one whose bold and bristling corollaries spread terror among hundreds of little girls in every direction. On the other hand, his simian arms, stilt-like legs, uncoordinated eyes, rosewood dentures, and schoolboy's ears gave the young marquis an unexpressed charm and an inexpressible attractiveness.

Tall in body and short on ideas, broad of chest but slight of wit, strong-shouldered but weak-minded, rich in brawn but poor in brain, he would assuredly enter the Kingdom of Heaven, either by piling mountains on top of each other, like Enceladus, or by living a strictly vegetable existence. [1]

Nevertheless, Anselme des Tilleuls enjoyed a well-deserved reputation when viewed from afar. Like tall buildings, he required some

---

1. Enceladus was a Titan struck down by Zeus and buried under Mt. Aetna.

distance in order to be seen to best advantage. At a hundred paces, he might have been taken for a pyramidal structure. At a hundred and fifty paces, he looked almost exactly like a kindly gentleman of high society. At two hundred paces he was an Antinous and the young ladies felt an unfamiliar palpitation agitate their maidenly chemisettes.[2] And at two hundred and fifty paces married women cast sinister looks at the husbands of their bosoms and racked their brains to find a way of reconciling the articles in the criminal and civil codes dealing with homicide and marriage.

But alas! The winding streets of the town of C…offered little opportunity for the young marquis to reach those flattering vantage points. And besides, how could one compromise a woman's reputation at such distances, or seduce young ladies with such a lack of proximity? How, in short, could one satisfy the most tender sentiments of the soul with someone a city block away?

And so, husbands and lovers slept between carefree sheets. They showered young Anselme with acts of kindness, and because of his personal purity, they voted unanimously to provide him with an alibi for philandering.

According to observations made at the bureau of longitudes, the Marquis des Tilleuls rose to a height of one meter ninety-five centimeters above sea level, whereas his intelligence was a good three meters below that of the stupidest cetacean. His only inferior as regards intellectual prowess was the sponge.

Now, Monsieur Anselme des Tilleuls claimed to be a marquis, neither more nor less, and a hereditary marquis at that. His was no recently conferred nobility! He had not laundered his inferior social rank in the government's wash-tub! He was neither peasant nor burgher, villain nor merchant, but a marquis in good standing.

His ancestor Rigobert, who had had sufficient nobility of spirit and greatness of soul to cure Louis the Stammerer of a severe case of indigestion in the year of grace 879, by using leaves from a *tilleul*, or linden tree, that cast its shadow on his little parcel of land, was ennobled on the spot by the relieved and grateful monarch.[3]

Since that memorable time, the Tilleul family had put down roots

---

2. Antinous was a handsome youth, a favorite of the Emperor Hadrian (76 - 138 A.D.)

3. Louis the Stammerer was Louis II, king of France from 877 to 879.

in their own backyard, paying no attention to foreign invasions or foreign events, and had made themselves as useless as possible to their respectable country.

During the defense of Paris by Eudes in 885, Rigobert des Tilleuls hid in his wine-cellar. [4]

At the time of the Crusades, Athanase des Tilleuls and his five sons simply folded their arms. [5]

Under Louis XI, in the days of the League of the Public Weal, Exupère des Tilleuls concerned himself with no one's weal but his own. [6]

When François I lost everything but his honor at the Battle of Pavia, Madame Aldégonde des Tilleuls, who was carrying on an affair with a young man, lost somewhat more than the King of France did. [7]

On the Day of the Barricades, the Tilleuls family built their barricades behind their own door, thereby setting an example seldom followed in our day. [8]

During the siege of Paris by Henri IV, at the depth of the great famine, Péréfixe des Tilleuls, far from having to eat his own children, fed them on provisions carefully hoarded in his miserly granaries. [9]

4. On November 26, 885, Norsemen with 700 drakkars (Viking longships) on the river Seine began an attack on Paris. The Count Eudes was the head of the resistance against the Norsemen.

5. As usual, Verne likes to play with words and double meanings of them. Here he uses the word "Croisades" (Crusades) and "se croiser les bras" (folding the arms, or crossing the arms, and doing nothing).

6. Louis XI (3 July 1423 – 30 August 1483), called the Prudent (French: *le Prudent*) and the Universal Spider (Middle French: *l'universelle aragne*) or the Spider King, was the King of France from 1461 to 1483. He was the son of Charles VII of France and Mary of Anjou, a member of the House of Valois, grandson of Charles VI and Isabeau of Bavaria and one of the most successful kings of France in terms of uniting the country. His 22-year reign was marked by political machinations, spinning a spider's web of plot and conspiracy which earned him his nickname. The League of the Public Weal was an alliance of feudal nobles organized in 1465 in defense of the centralized authority of King Louis XI.

7. Fought on 24 February 1525, the Battle of Pavia was the decisive battle of the Italian war, in which the Habsburg Emperor Charles V defeated King François I of France.

8. On 12 May 1588, the Catholic population of Paris erected barricades against King Henri III.

9. After the death of King Henri III, his brother, Henri of Navarre, marched on Paris,

Under Richelieu, the descendants of this illustrious lineage took advantage of the disturbances to live in perfect peace, and during the war with Holland Népomucène des Tilleuls waged war only on the rats that were eating his Dutch cheeses. [10]

During the Seven Years War, Madame Frédégonde des Tilleuls gave birth to seven lovely children. Unless her virtue is to be questioned, it must be assumed that Aglibert des Tilleuls, her valiant husband, did not spend those years fighting Frederick the Great alongside Marshal de Saxe.[11]

In the end, these choice aristocrats were not noble enough to fall under suspicion in '93, but sufficiently noble to collect their share of reparations after the return of the Bourbons. [12]

And so Anselme des Tilleuls, the last of that name, walked in the footsteps of his illustrious forefathers. He was not handsome, or brave, or overly generous, but ignorant, cowardly, and foolish. He was, in a word, a marquis, a genuine marquis, by the grace of God and the indigestion of Louis the Stammerer.

In 1842 he was still studying Latin with a respectable professor, one Naso Paraclet, a man well-versed in the study of the Latin tongue and whose entire intelligence was evaluated at three hundred crowns per annum. [13]

He was young Anselme's spiritual director, the strait-laced mentor of a Telemachus in the skin of a marquis, for the orphaned pupil could see, hear, and understand nothing that exceeded the intellectual powers of his professor. [14]

Naso Paraclet's speech was imbued with the chaste tranquility that was the distinguishing feature of his favorite hero, the pious Aeneas.[15]

---

touching off a civil war as a result of which he was crowned King Henri IV.

10. Cardinal de Richelieu (1585-1642) was one of the most powerful men in France, as Prime Minister of King Louis XIII. Richelieu is a main character of Alexandre Dumas's *The Three Musketeers*. France and Holland were at war from 1672 to 1678.

11. The Marshal de Saxe was the French military commander during the War of the Austrian Succession (1740-1748). He died in 1750, before the outbreak of the Seven Years War (1756-1765).

12. During and after the Reign of Terror.

13. Naso was one of the names of the Roman poet Ovid: Publius Ovidius Naso. The Paraclete is a name for the Holy Spirit (see Preface).

14. Telemachus was the son of Ulysses and Penelope.

15. In Greco-Roman mythology, Aeneas (Greek: Αἰνείας) was a Trojan hero, the

His sentences were liberally sprinkled with phrases and examples taken from the Latin grammar of Lhomond, professor emeritus at the former University of Paris. [16]

"By the doe's belly, Monsieur le Marquis," the pious Paraclet would say to him frankly, "you belong to a nobility that is as old as it is ancient, and you will make your way in life, or, as we say in Latin, *Viam facietis* (for I would not take the liberty of speaking familiarly to you in that divine, but dishonest, tongue)."

"Be that as it may," the pathetic Anselme would reply, "I have now reached the full age of twenty-seven. "Perhaps it may be high time for me to be initiated into the secrets of the world."

"*Cupidus videndi.*[17] Your rules of conduct and grammar are all to be found in Lhomond. From *Deus sanctus* all the way to *Virtus et vitium contraria*, the lofty principles of syntax and morality are clearly explained and deduced." [18]

"But after all," young Anselme went on, "there must surely be a suitable marriage in store to guarantee the continuation of my nearly extinct family."

"There is no doubt, Monsieur le Marquis, that on you rest the hopes of a noble lineage. *Domus inclinata recumbit.*" [19]

"*Recumbit humi bos*," ventured des Tilleuls, to show off his knowledge. [20]

---

son of prince Anchises and the goddess Aphrodite. His father was also the second cousin of King Priam of Troy. The journey of Aeneas from Troy (led by Aphrodite, his mother), which led to the founding of the city of Rome, is recounted in Virgil's *Aeneid*. He is considered an important figure in Greek and Roman legend and history.

16. Abbé Charles-François Lhomond (1727-1794) a French grammarian (see Preface).

17. "Eager to see" (Lhomond's Grammar, page 136).

18. *Deus sanctus*: "God is holy" (Lhomond's Grammar, page 133). *Virtus et vitium contraria*: "Virtue and vice are opposites."

19. "The faltering house rests on you" (Lhomond's Grammar, page 134). *Domus inclinata recumbit* is the end of Line 59 of Book XII of Virgil's *Aeneid*. The complete quote is *in te omnis domus inclinata recumbit*, which means "our whole faltering house rests on you." In Virgil's *Aeneid*, the line becoming extinct is that of King Latinus and his wife, Amata.

20. *"Recumbit humi bos,"*: "The ox lies on the ground." Here Anselme des Tilleuls incorrectly quotes Virgil, whose line 481 of Book V of the *Aeneid* is *Procumbit*

"A thousand pardons, my illustrious pupil, but you are confusing two words. *Procumbit humi bos* means 'the ox falls to the ground,' and is used by Virgil in a different context. *Domus inclinata recumbit*, translated word for word, means as follows: *domus*, your family, *imclinata*, on the verge of extinction, *recumbit*, rests on you alone."

"But who will ever fall in love with me, my good Paraclet?"

"Do you not have an income of forty thousand livres? Since when does anyone refuse to marry forty thousand livres, offered by twenty-seven noble years, together with the title of marquis in good standing, when that title keeps its wealth under the vast paneling of a dungeoned castle? One would have to be mad, or else have an income of forty-one thousand francs."

"But actually," went on the marquis, "what is marriage?"

"Monsieur," replied Paraclet innocently, "it is something of which I have never availed myself. I have been a bachelor lo these fifty-one years, and never has my mind, even in a dream, caught a glimpse of conjugal bliss, *attamen*, insofar as it is permissible for an honest man, *vir bonus dicendi peritus*, to make a rough guess about things with which he is not familiar, *de re aut visu, aut auditu, aut tactu*, (and that latter phrase is a forceful expression of my thinking), I shall answer Monsieur le Marquis des Tilleuls to the best of my ability, since it is my duty to inculcate in him the basic principles of society, up to and including its procreation." [21]

The professor thought he was going to suffocate after that long sentence, but fortunately he blew his nose, took out his snuff box, which was decorated with a portrait of Virgil dressed in black and wearing the cross of the Legion of Honor, inserted a gram of snuff into his eager nostril with a practiced thumb, and continued.

"I am the pious Naso Paraclet, and I shall impart to you, Monsieur le Marquis, my personal observations about that anti-Gordian knot known as marriage, hymen, or *matrimonium*. Lhomond, in his course

---

humi bos, exactly what Paraclet says in the next sentence: "the bull falls quivering on the ground" (transl. H.R. Fairclough).

21. *Attamen*: "However." *Vir bonus dicendi peritus*: "An honest man, skilful in speech." This is the definition of a speaker by Cato the Elder (Marcus Porcius Cato, 234 – 149 B.C.), a Roman statesman, surnamed the Censor (*Censorius*), the Wise (*Sapiens*), the Ancient (*Priscus*), or the Elder (*Maior*), to distinguish him from Cato the Younger (his great-grandson). *De re aut visu, aut auditu, aut tactu*: "Neither in fact, by sight, by hearing, or by touch."

on moral philosophy by example, proposes to begin by conjugating the verb *amo*, I love. There is in the choice of that word a certain subtlety which may possibly be missed at first glance, but which at second glance is missed altogether. Let us proceed by using both the synthetic and analytic methods simultaneously. What is the meaning of *amo*?

"I love," replied the young Anselme cheerfully.

"And what part of speech is it?"

"A verb."

"Is it active, passive, intransitive, or deponent?"

"Active," was the instant reply.

"Yes, it is active, and I emphasize that essential quality," said the professor, warming to his subject. "It is active, and in order to govern the accusative case, it must be active, sometimes deponent, but never passive or intransitive. To continue, when a verb is not in the infinitive, what then?"

"It agrees with its nominative, or subject."

"Admirable, my noble pupil. You may be sure that the twenty-seven years of your youth have not been wasted. It agrees with the nominative, or subject. Well then, do you know what you are, Monsieur le Marquis? You are a subject, a good subject, an excellent subject, a brilliant subject. As such, you are the nominative of the sentence, the individual named—and well named—Anselme des Tilleuls. *Ergo!*[22] You are in command of the entire sentence. What is a sentence? It is the image of life, with its disappointments and commas, its phrases and hopes, its pleasures and exclamation marks. *Ergo!* You, the subject, control at your pleasure everything that the sentence contains within itself, from the first adverb to the last preposition, and you act, necessarily and through an intermediary, on the direct object. I say 'through an intermediary' because between you and that object stands the indispensible verb, the action which, once set in motion by the subject, brings the object inevitably under its control."

"But what is that verb?," asked young Anselme, his interest rising.

"That verb?" It is the verb *amo*, I love, the essentially active verb which governs—what? The accusative case. For example, I love God *amo Deum*. The object is subordinate to the verb and hence to the subject."

"What is the object, then?"

22. "Therefore." (Lhomond's Grammar, page 96)

"Here," said the pious Naso, blushing, give me your full attention, my noble pupil. In the syntax of society, there are said to be three distinct genders, just as there are in the Latin language. You belong essentially to the masculine gender, since you were registered as such at your local municipal office. But other individuals are neuter, like Origen, Abelard, etc., and, like neuter, or intransitive verbs, do not enjoy the pleasure of having an object in the accusative case.[23] For example, I study grammar, *studeo grammaticae.*[24] Finally, the feminine gender makes its appearance, and that is what concerns us now. Woman, I have been told, belongs to that last category. She is readily recognizable by her customary apparel and her completely beardless chin. Made essentially to be governed, to remain under the direct action of the subject and the verb, she always is and always must be in the accusative, with its accentuated shapes. What, then, joins the subject to the object, the nominative to the accusative, the man to the woman? The verb, the active, very active verb, as active as it can possibly be, the verb so frequently found in the fourth book of the *Aeneid* (which, out of modesty, I have had you omit), this verb, this hyphen joining Aeneas to the Queen of Carthage. *Aeneas amat Didonem.*[25]. Marriage is the

23. Origen (Greek: Ὠριγένης, or Origen Adamantius, c. 185–254) was an early Christian scholar and theologian, and one of the most distinguished of the early fathers of the Christian Church, whose religious zeal led him to castrate himself. Pierre Abélard (1079 – 1142) was a medieval French scholastic philosopher, theologian and preeminent logician. He was castrated for having had a love affair and correspondence with Héloise d'Argenteuil (1101 – 1164), French nun, writer, scholar, and abbess. The *Letters of Héloise and Abelard* are a classic of world literature.

24. "I study grammar" (Lhomond's Grammar, page 146). This example shows that the verb *studere,* to study, is intransitive (or "neuter"), since it is followed by an indirect object in the dative case, rather than a direct object in the accusative.

25. "Aeneas loves Dido." According to Virgil's *Aeneid*, Dido, also called Elissa, was princess of Tyre in Phoenicia. Escaping tyranny in her country, she came to Libya where she founded Carthage, a great city which Aeneas and his comrades, who had become refugees after the sack of Troy, visited seven years after the end of the Trojan War. As Queen of Carthage, she received the Trojan exiles with hospitality, and having given Aeneas more love than he could take, felt betrayed when he left for Italy, and committed suicide. *Dido and Aeneas* is an English tragedy opera in three acts by the Baroque composer Henry Purcell (ca. 1659 – 1695). The libretto was written by Nahum Tate in English, based on the *Aeneid* of Virgil. It premiered in London, at Josias Priest's School for Young Gentlewomen, on December 1689. The setting is in Carthage after the Trojan War.

conjugation of this verb, from the honey-filled present to the bitter infinitive. Conjugate to your heart's content, Monsieur le Marquis. In life, as in syntax, there are four conjugations. Some are distinguished by their momentum and their imperative, others by their intoxication and their supine, others again by their effervescence and their gerundive, ending in *dus, da, dum.* Conjugate, noble des Tilleuls, conjugate!

"*Amo, amas, amat, amamus,*" said the young Anselme obediently, hearing the furnaces of his heart roar at the vehement utterance of those amorous descriptions. [26]

"Very good, Monsieur le Marquis," said the professor, mopping his streaming brow. "One last word of advice, and we shall be on our way to Cythera." [27]

"Speak, learned Naso."

"Take care not to admit a pronoun into your sentence. Your accusative would be in the gravest danger, for the pronoun always takes the place of the noun or subject."

Thoroughly edified by this conjugal and grammatical discussion, young Anselme des Tilleuls racked his brain night and day in an effort to reach the underlying layers concealing the tenderest of mysteries. If the truth be told, however, he did not rack his brains very far, for his poorly tempered faculties were soon shattered on the rock of unintelligence. Naso Paraclet pursued still further his study of the principles of all moral philosophy, buried deep in grammar. He devoted himself successfully to the moral cultivation of the fig leaf, and made useful comments about irregular Latin declensions.

The town of C..., where these illustrious individuals lived, had a population of about seven thousand, but intellectually speaking, it contained at most two hundred souls, including the souls of animals.

This provincial town, with its narrow streets and narrow minds, rose at six o'clock in the morning and retired at nine o'clock in the evening, following the example of its feathered barnyard guests. During the day it went about its very ordinary business, having breakfast at nine and dining at four. It was a town unfettered by remorse or civilization. It laced itself up in the front, bared itself down to the chin, wore black stockings and dark-colored shoes, traveled about on broad feet and

---

26. *Amo, amas, amat, amamus:* "I love, you love, he (she) loves, we love" (Lhomond's Grammar, page 32).

27. Birthplace of Aphrodite, the goddess of love and beauty.

clapped with even broader hands when it applauded home-grown virtuosos. Leg-of-mutton sleeves puffed out around its arms, its hats possessed an anti-adulterous virtue, and its marriageable daughters, who used sturdy whalebone stays to hold back the avalanche of their charms, were the possessors of genuine chastity belts. When the townsfolk went to visit the local notables after nightfall, they lighted their way with the proverbial lantern, their wooden shoes clattering over the sharp-cornered paving stones. [28]

But during these indescribable soirées, the mammals did not intermingle indiscriminately. The nobility kept to themselves, crushing the burghers under the hundredweight burdens of their provincial arrogance. And yet, very few of those worthy aristocrats could compare their genealogical titles with the time-worn parchments of the Marquis des Tilleuls. Not everyone is fortunate enough to have ancestors who enjoyed both social success and success as an apothecary during the reign of Louis the Stammerer.

Nevertheless, despite the quantities of ugliness so prodigally bestowed on the inhabitants of C…, young Anselme was considered a double prodigy, because of the imperfection of his features and the incompetence of his mind. The only one who came close was Naso, who even made so bold as to find something distinguished about him. To hear him talk, one would have to be senile not to find his pupil attractive at last glance, and he invited his detractors to take a walk in the fields playing the clarinet – *ite clarinettam lusum.*[29] What is more, he used the supine, in view of the motions and contortions required to play that nasal-sounding instrument.

Now the pious Paraclet had undertaken the responsibility of getting his pupil suitably established, and he knew that he was made of flesh and blood, like anyone else. It must not be assumed that because

---

28. Verne refers to the French popular expression *éclairer la lanterne* ("light the lantern"), still in use today. The origin of this expression can be found in a fable, *Le Singe et la lanterne magique* ("The Monkey and the Magic Lantern"), by Jean-Pierre Claris de Florian (1755-1794), a French poet and novelist. In the fable, a monkey invites his friends to a magic lantern show, but forgets to turn on the lantern.

29. "Go play the clarinet." Verne mixes the so-called (in French) *latin de cuisine* ("kitchen Latin") used by students to make jokes and word plays with Lhomond's Grammar "official," "true" Latin. It's obvious that clarinets didn't exist during Roman times, when Latin was a spoken language!

Anselme felt nothing, understood very little and loved even less, his feelings were therefore simply chimeras or myths. No, his soul could be as easily crushed as anyone else's. He had kept the powder of his heart dry, and a mere phosphoric friction might cause it to explode suddenly, covering the virgin surroundings with burning debris.

That was why Naso egged on his pupil's passion and destroyed many drumheads in leading him to the attack. Every morning he thought he heard the young marquis say, "Pious Paraclet, what is this terrible insomnia that torments me?" *Anna soror, quae me suspensam insomnia terrent?* which he translated freely to himself as "Sister Anne, sister Anne, do you not see anything coming?[30]

But since the sun was shining hazily and the grass was growing green in the stony imagination of this granite-like character, the good professor acted quietly. He mounted a campaign to win the fecund fiancée who would rescue the des Tilleuls family from imminent extinction. Compared to this undertaking, Alexander the Great's marches were a Midsummer Day's outing. Naso ignored none of the dangers of his expedition. He steeped his soul in legendary tales of ancient victories by rereading Xenophon and Thucydides night and day, until the retreat of the Ten Thousand seemed like a master stroke of strategy.[31]

---

30. Anna was the legendary sister of Dido. More correct translations of this line 9 of Book IV of Virgil's *Aeneid* are: "Sister Anne, what sights fill me with terror and anguish?" or "Sister Anna, what dreams torment me, hung up (with anxiety)!" or "Anna, my sister, what dreams thrill me with fears?"

31. Xenophon (ca. 430 - 354 B.C.), also known as Xenophon of Athens, was a soldier, mercenary, and a contemporary and admirer of Socrates. He is known for his writings on the history of his own times, preserving the sayings of Socrates, and the life of ancient Greece. *The Anabasis* (Ἀνάβασις - Greek for "going up") is his most famous. The journey it narrates is his best known accomplishment and "one of the great adventures in human history," according to Will Durant. Xenophon accompanied the Ten Thousand, a large army of Greek mercenaries hired by Cyrus the Younger, who intended to seize the throne of Persia from his brother, Artaxerxes II. Though Cyrus's mixed army fought to a tactical victory in Babylon (401 B.C.), Cyrus himself was killed in the battle, rendering the actions of the Greeks irrelevant and the expedition a failure. Like Xenophon, Thucydides (ca. 460 – ca. 395 B.C.) was a Greek historian and author of the *History of the Peloponnesian War*, which recounts the 5th century B.C. war between Sparta and Athens to the year 411 B.C. Thucydides has been dubbed the father of "scientific history" due to his strict standards of evidence-gathering and analysis in terms of cause and effect without reference to intervention by the gods, as outlined in

But he was great-hearted and his love was immense. Nothing daunted, he set up camp within cannon range of the neighboring heiresses. It can be truly said that he had covered his rear with the support of the des Tilleuls family tree and protected his attack with the eight thousand hundred-sou pieces that made up the young marquis's income.

"By Jupiter," he said to himself, "who could withstand such attacks as these? Madame Mirabelle and her five marriageable daughters? Or Monsieur de Pertinax, the President of the Tribunal, who is said to be the possessor of a most exceptional accusative? Or General de Vieille Pierre, who does not know with what nominative he should make his daughter and heir agree? In the houses one meets whole declensions of unemployed daughters. Who would not want to unite with the noble blood of the des Tilleuls? Where, I say, is the miller who would not trade his mill for a bishop's miter? *Sic parvis componere magna solebam.*[32]

So it was that, while the young Marquis Anselme, now in the prime of life at the age of twenty-seven, was concentrating the nocturnal rays of his intelligence on the rule governing the untranslated *que,* the pious Naso was mounting his regenerative hobby-horse and spurring full tilt towards the souls of the young heiresses.

Anselme was entering into the spirit of the language of Ausonius, and Naso into that of Madame de Mirabelle. [33] The marquis was identifying with the genius of Lhomond, while Paraclet was using all his genius to open matrimonial paths among nubile hearts.

Madame de Mirabelle was an elderly widow, who always wore the same green, leaf-patterned gown. She was tall, thin, dry, and bad-tempered. In her presence, one could not help thinking of the bean poles sticking up on the plains of Champagne.

A few inhabitants of C…, with lower-class views, continued to say that M. de Mirabelle had quickly worn out his life on the rough edges of his angular wife.

Be that as it may, their stormy marriage had produced five daughters.

---

his introduction to his work. It seems that Naso Parclet, fluent in Latin, was also able to read Greek.

32. "Thus I was in the habit of comparing great things with small."

33. Decimius Magnus Ausonius (ca. 310–395) was a Latin poet and rhetorician, born at Burdigala (today: Bordeaux, France), in the Roman Province of Gaul.

These respectable young ladies, ranging in age from twenty to twenty-five winters, were all unmarried. Their mother announced their marital status whenever she brought them out into society, and the young men fluttered about, in danger of getting their coat-tails burned, while the young ladies waved their silk nets about, worrying that they might never catch even one butterfly.

Nevertheless, each of them boasted of her hundred-thousand-franc dowry, and winked brazenly with the most mercenary of intentions. Their multicolored eyes, like Iris's sash, formed a battery of ten Leyden jars, containing many attractive bits of quivering gold leaf. [34] Alas! Not one well-to-do young man had been smitten by the violence of their electrical shock, and they all still had their electricity bills to pay.

The fact is that they all looked more or less like their mother, and their mother had an unpleasant profile.

What a setback might be in store, then, for the pious Naso when, like the valet Landry, he took on this five of hearts?

And so, clad in a black coat whose tails voluptuously caressed his nervous ankles, a formal vest with shimmering spangles, and trousers that stopped unpardonably short of the shining buckles on his shoes, the bold Paraclet ventured forth among those virgins, whom the moon seemed to have overlooked when distributing its honey. He felt out the terrain, estimated the emptiness of those tearful souls by their vague sighs, and put forward his request in carefully chosen terms.

The way those young faces lit up in the rays of the conjugal sun did not surprise him. An infinite number of wishes, multiplied by five, were about to be fulfilled. Every morning, the misunderstood daughters bemoaned their fate, hoping for this happy day and uttering, among them, a total of one thousand eight hundred and twenty-five sighs per year.

"Yes, ladies," said the pious Naso, "he is a young man with a sure future and a commendable past. His is the newest of all available hearts, and his soul is innocent of any burning emotion. He is a virginal lamp that I myself have filled with new oil. I have trimmed it with care, and it awaits only a suitable flame in order to burn with an inextinguishable fire."

---

34. Iris was the goddess of the rainbow, the messenger of the Olympian gods. She was often represented as the handmaiden and personal messenger of Hera. Iris was a goddess of sea and sky, her father Thaumas "the wondrous" was a marine-god, and her mother Elektra "the amber" a cloud-nymph.

"And is he handsome?" asked the young ladies, as harmoniously as a village choir.

"Ladies, he is not handsome; he is magnificent."

"And is he rich?" asked the mother, keeping up, in her intelligent way, the tenor of the conversation.

"He is not rich, madame, he is a millionaire."

"Is he witty?" continued the young virgins.

"He is witty enough to delight a woman."

"And his name is…?"

"If I had been Tityrus[35], you would have said *Sed tamen, iste Deus, qui sit, da Tityre, nobis.*[36] Introduce us to this God, whoever he may be."

"Well, then?" exclaimed the mother and her daughters with one voice.

"The Marquis Anselme des Tilleuls!"

The marquis's frightful ugliness and the fear of marrying him brought about a visible change.

The eldest daughter fainted. The second collapsed in nervous prostration. The third swooned. The fourth fell flat on her back. The fifth fell flat on her face. The mother was completely flabbergasted.[37]

As they fell, one after the other, the good professor was reminded of the houses of cards he used to make as a child. He could have taken advantage of his position to undo all those fainting fits, but, eminently chaste as he was, he took his courage in one hand, his hat in the other, and left, saying *"Ipse gravis graviterque ad terram pondere vasto concidit.*[38]

But the pious Naso was big-hearted and those human prostrations were beneath him. He went back to his pupil, feigning an air of sardonic stoicism.

---

35. The name comes from the first line of Virgil's first *Eclogue*, "*Titure tu patulae recubans sub tegmine fagi*" (Tityre Tus loved to lurk in the dark night looking for mischief).

36. Verse 18 of Virgil's *First Eclogue*.

37. Again Verne plays with words and uses the word "tomber" (falling) in all five sentences. A literal translation would be: "The eldest daughter fell in a faint." "The second fell into nervous prostration." "The third fell in a swoon." "The fourth fell flat on her back." "The fifth fell flat on her face, and the mother fell down from the high clouds."

38. "He himself fell heavily to the ground with all his weight, a heavy mass." Line 498 of Book V of Virgil's *Aeneid. Concidit* is the first word of the next line.

There is, however, reason to believe that, if he had had a tail, he would not have been holding it erect.[39]

Anselme des Tilleuls was sitting hunched over his syntax. Perhaps the object of this laborious obstinacy was to calm his burning passion. No doubt the erotic female images of the Latin language were affecting his brain, and the ardor of his blood was calmed by the peculiarly anti-aphrodisiac contemplation of the mysteries of the untranslated *que*.

"Well," said the last heir to the des Tilleuls name, "what say the Mirabelle ladies?"

"Translate this word for word," replied Paraclet. "*Mira*, admire, *belle*, with care, the family to which you belong, Monsieur le Marquis, and do not marry beneath you. These are ladies of the lower nobility, small-minded and small in fortune, and you would never have anything but small children. To have *petits-enfants* is the prerogative of *grands-parents*."

"Alas!" moaned Anselme.

"Take heart, my noble pupil. After the verbs 'advise,' 'persuade,' etc., how is 'that' or 'to' translated?"

"It is translated by '*ut*' with the subjunctive."

"I shall give you a good mark for that answer. I am now on my way to see General de Vieille Pierre."

No sooner said than done. Anselme went on with his homework and Naso Paraclet, dressed as before, ventured forth with melancholy steps toward the lovely Amaltulde.

She was the general's daughter and the apple of his eye. Every day her father offered wholesale sacrifices on the altar of her whims.

In physical appearance, this sprightly lass was full-bodied, broad-shouldered, wide-hipped, lively in her movements, and sturdy of limb. She was bold in character, with a petulant brusqueness and an uncontrollable temperament. She wore a képi on her head and her dress was a flag riddled with holes. She had the right build for carrying a haversack and needed no encouragement to charge into battle. Her father, who had defeated enemy battalions, was himself defeated, and retreated before his daughter's every wish. She was an Amazon, but without the bow and the mutilation necessary for its use. In a word, she had army rations in her blood. [40]

---

39. Verne's typical scatological humor.

40. Amazon women were said to cut off their right breast so that it would not obstruct their use of a bow in warfare.

It would have taken a combination of Ajax and Achilles to stand up to that young woman. She could easily have been mistaken for a fortress, with its machicolations, its barbicans, and its mangonels. She looked like a cannon loaded with grapeshot.

The pious Naso, with no other armor than his conscience, put his trust in God and in Lhomond, his prophet of the Latin tongue.

He had to plan the siege carefully, preparing escape routes and laying mines. As for trenches, the good professor already had enough of those, produced by an uncontrollable fear. But his mind was made up. Sounding the charge and jingling his gold coins, he presented himself at the general's barracks.

He was greeted by a dog dressed as a doorman and, at his urgent request, was ushered into the presence of the noble Amaltulde de Vieille Pierre.

History has left no record of this memorable encounter, during which, in the presence of the general and his daughter, Paraclet asked for her valiant hand on behalf of his beloved pupil.

No one knows whether it was really the hand that was given to him on that occasion, or to what part of his body it was applied. Suffice it to say that after a five-minute parliamentary explanation, the professor beat a hasty retreat, abandoning his project and his hat on the field of battle. In a few short moments, he had come under enemy fire, wiped the sweat from his brow, dusted off the seat of his trousers, and suffered a major setback.[41]

His precipitate flight deposited him promptly in front of the portcullis of the des Tilleuls castle. With measured tread he mounted the seigniorial stairway and reached the young marquis's room.

He found him in tears, staring at the list of verbs that are in the indicative in French, but which must be put in the subjunctive in Latin.

"My dear pupil, what is the matter, sir?" asked Naso, deeply concerned.

"Good professor," replied Anselme, "when the expression 'how much' comes between two verbs, must the second always be in the subjunctive?"

---

41. Verne here plays with the word "essuyer" (to wipe out). A literal translation would be: "In a few short moments, he just wiped out the fire of his enemies, the sweat of his brow, the bottom of his trousers, and huge reverses." He uses here the same writing technique as mentioned in note 66.

"Exactly."

"For example," continued Anselme, "you see how much I love you, *vides quantum te amem*." [42]

"Bravo, Monsieur le Marquis! That particular use is a melancholy one. Please go on."

"*Vides quantum te amem.* Already I seem to hear Mademoiselle de Vieille Pierre singing that soft refrain to me."

Without batting an eyelid, Naso asked, in his most professorial voice, "To indicate how long something has been going on, in what case is the noun expressing time?"

"In the accusative."

"Good! For example?"

"I have been a friend of your father's for many years," replied Anselme. "*multos annos utor familiariter patre tuo.*" [43]

"Yes, Monsieur le Marquis," replied the clever Paraclet, "I was a close friend of your father's, and he considered himself above the military kind of nobility, which depends on the point of a sword. Furthermore, if the reference is to past time, the noun must be in the ablative case with *abhinc*. [44] For example?"

"He died three years ago," replied the last of the des Tilleuls, "*tres abhinc annis mortuus est.*"

"Yes, Monsieur le Marquis, three years, and his dying wishes still reverberate in my memory. Now the daughter of a warrior is not worthy to mingle her new race with the antiquity of yours, nor to tie her charger to the noble branches of the des Tilleuls. If you accept her hand, I believe you will regret it, or, as it says in the grammar textbook, *credo fore ut te pœniteret*. [45] I am now off to visit the president of the court of first instance. Meanwhile, in connection with our grammatical and matrimonial research, in a case where the Latin verb has no future infinitive, you will keep repeating, *credo fore ut brevi illud negotium confecerit*, I believe he will soon have finished this business."

Thereupon the pious Naso left his pupil and, drawing from the

---

42. Lhomond's Grammar, page 211.

43. Lhomond's Grammar, page 181.

44. "Since" (Lhomond's Grammar, page 181).

45. Lhomond's Grammar, page 200.

cistern of adversity the boiling water of courage, took heart and set off to confront the town's first magistrate.

Proh pudor.[46] He was demeaning himself. He was clothing the marquis's illustrious forebears in a black gown and a dark cap. Naso Paraclet's behavior resembled that of the heron in La Fontaine's fable. After turning up his nose at the carps and tenches of the high aristocracy, he now had to settle for snails, or heiresses of lower rank.

Monsieur de Pertinax, like many Parisian and provincial judges, took his siesta while sitting in his armchair at the tribunal. Surrounded by the pleasures of magisterial indolence, and assisted by judicial drowsiness, he digested the court proceedings—and his breakfast—in leisurely fashion.

The pious Naso had heard that he was the proud father of a charming daughter, although he had never even set eyes on her. The first magistrate was an uncommunicative kind of man and kept himself shut up in an inaccessible retreat.

According to the local gossips, the young lady was being educated in one of the best boarding schools in the capital, and heaven had endowed her with surpassing beauty.

But these rumors rarely floated through the town, and it would have taken a skilful news hunter to hit them with the small shot of curiosity.

But Naso had several trophies in his game bag. He estimated that the young lady had a reasonable fortune, and that her father's aristocratic prejudices were as high as the pyramids. Confidence had therefore dried his tears when, at the end of a hearing, he approached the stern Monsieur de Pertinax.

The impartial magistrate had just finished a famous case in which both parties came out the losers. The debtor had been ordered to pay his debt to the creditor, and the latter had to pay the costs, which came to twice the amount of the debt.

The honorable president enjoyed the inestimable appearance of a man whose conscience and stomach regularly neglected to cry out. With a sweeping, dignified gesture, he invited Naso to explain the object of his visit.

---

46. "Shame" (Lhomond's Grammar, page 97).

"Monsieur le President," said the confident professor, "it concerns a hand in marriage and a capital affair on which the safety of society depends."

"Go on, sir. I am bursting with curiosity."

"I have every reason to think so, Monsieur de Pertinax."

"Do you wish me to summon the attorney general for this communication?"

"There is no need to disturb the minister. My explanation will be brief, for indolence is not permissible. *Non mihi licit est pigro.*"[47]

"Do go on, Monsieur…Monsieur…"

"Naso Paraclet, professor of Latin and other languages, future successor to Lhomond and member of the General Council on Public Education for children below the age of seven."

"That is good enough," said Monsieur de Pertinax, bowing.

"Monsieur," continued Paraclet with his most ingratiating smile, "I am connected by a double bond, as both teacher and friend, to the richest man in this town, *ditissimus urbis,* and without any question the most notable of all, *maxime omnium conspicuus.* The abolition of aristocratic privileges has deeply affected my heart, for that brilliant entourage surrounded the old throne with a protective halo. I am one of the soldiers, *unus militum,* or *ex militibus,* or *inter milites* (for a partitive noun requires that a plural following it should be in the genitive case, or in the ablative with *ex,* or in the accusative with *inter*). I am, as I was saying, one of the soldiers of that little army of brave souls who will save society by restoring its noblest institutions. For a great disaster threatens us, *magna calamitas nobis imminet, impendet, instat.*"[48]

"Go on, sir," said the somewhat astonished president.

"My young pupil," went on the elegant professor, "is extremely wealthy and lacks for nothing, *abundant divitiis, nulla re caret.*[49] Now you, Monsieur le President, have in your family a noble offspring. Need I ask you whether you love your children? *Quænam mater liberos suos non amat?*"[50]

---

47. "I am not permitted to be lazy" (Lhomond's Grammar, page 135).

48. In this paragraph, Verne almost copied a whole page of Lhomond's grammar. Lhomond uses *Maxime omnium conspicuus* to explain the rules of partitive nouns and the three ways to express "I am one of the soldiers" (Lhomond's Grammar, page 143).

49. Lhomond's Grammar, page 149.

50. "What mother, I ask you, does not love her own children?"

Monsieur de Pertinax nodded in agreement.

"Now my pupil, Monsieur Anselme des Tilleuls, a hereditary marquis, has fallen into the abyss of melancholy, and I am overcome with grief, *mœrore conficior.*[51] I did not know how to account for his morose condition, but I had to acknowledge that love had something to do with it. *Teneo lupum auribus*, I said to myself in French.[52] I must find him a wife. I know that crowds of heiresses rush up to him, *turba ruit* or *ruunt.*[53] But only one woman in the world had stabilized the weathervane of his uncertainty. I found out the name of that heaven-sent woman. It was your daughter, Monsieur de Pertinax. Since then you have been the object of my attentive investigation. I saw your house, *vidi domun tuam*, and I admired its beauty, *et illius pulchritudinem miratus sum.*"[54]

"Are you saying that this young nobleman loves my daughter?" asked the president with a smile. "Or, to put it in your own language, *dicis hunc juvenem amare filiam meam?*"

"No, Monsieur," said Naso hotly. "That would be a syntactical error. The active voice must be replaced by the passive when there is ambiguity, in other words, when the French subject and object, following an untranslated *que*, are both in the accusative case in Latin and cannot be distinguished one from the other. For example, to translate 'You say that Anselme des Tilleuls loves my daughter', as *Dicis Anselmem ex Tiliis amare filiam meam* is incorrect. The sentence must be rephrased to read 'You say that my daughter is loved by Anselme des Tilleuls', *Dicis filiam meam amari ab Anselme ex Tiliis.*"[55]

"Be that as it may, Monsieur Paraclet, I fear that it will be an unrequited love."

"Monsieur," the professor retorted heatedly, "we have been nobility since the time of Louis the Stammerer. We have an income of forty

---

51. Lhomond's Grammar, page 156. In the manuscript, Verne underlines this Latin expression. Usually he writes them italicized.

52. "I am in an awkward situation." (Lhomond's Grammar, page 181) (Literally, I am holding the wolf by the ears.)

53. Literally, the crowd (singular) rushes up or the people (plural) rush up (Lhomond's Grammar, page 145).

54. Lhomond's Grammar, page 169.

55. Here again Verne uses a mix of correct Latin and the so-called *latin de cuisine* (kitchen Latin). It's hard to imagine Anselme used as a first name in Ancient Rome.

thousand livres. In the name of heaven and the faltering monarchies, what is the meaning of this refusal?"

"It means that I have no daughter. I only have a son," said Monsieur de Pertinax.

"And what does that matter, sir?"

"But you are making a very strange mistake."

"True," said Naso in a piteous voice. "I am being carried away by my patriotism. Why is your son not a daughter? But perhaps there is a cure for that."

"None that I can see," replied the first magistrate.[56]

"Sir," said Paraclet, "you seem to be busy at the moment. We shall resume this serious conversation later."

"But I tell you again, I only have a son. It is impossible for your marquis to marry him."

"Indeed, at first glance it appears difficult, but…"

"Your 'buts' make no sense."

"Does my proposition violate any articles in the Criminal Code?" added the persistent Paraclet.

"None."

"Well, then?"

"Sir," said the judge, turning purple, "must I call my ushers to show you out?"

"*Quis te furor tenet*?[57] Say nothing about this matter," said Naso angrily.

"If you do not leave at once," shouted the crimson-faced judge, "I shall call out the departmental gendarmes."

"You are not your normal self. We shall discuss this matter later."

"Get out!" roared the judge, turning white as chalk, "or I shall send for the national guard."

---

56. In 1898 Hetzel published *Le Superbe Orénoque* (*The Mighty Orinoco*), a novel by Jules Verne which had to wait more than a century before being translated into English. Like most of the Vernian novels, *The Mighty Orinoco* is an initiatory adventure on top of a geographical itinerary. The geographical part is in South America, as indicated by the title. But the initiatory adventure is the question of gender: is the hero a woman or a man? Even if it's done in a hilarious way here, through the dialog between Paracelet and Monsieur de Pertinax, the very modern gender question was already in Verne's mind.

57. "What madness possesses you?"

"*Te relinquo*," cried Paraclet angrily and in Latin.[58] "But I will have more to say about this, and my pupil will marry into your family."

The first magistrate of C…was about to resort to physical violence when the obstinate professor left the building and flew into a rage that changed from red to purple to white. Several times he uttered a thunderous *Quos ego*, which was answered by rebellious echoes directed at the subjects of Neptune.[59]

Paraclet had been wounded in his haughty schemes. He used the energetic phrases of Cicero in his monologue, and his anger, finding its source in the lofty mountains of Pride, sent down its streams of insults and its torrents of invective between the abusive banks of *quousque tandem*[60] and *verum enimvero.*[61]

He walked along, waving his arms like a busy semaphore and wondering whether his pupil should not take revenge for Monsieur de Pertinax's refusal, which was based on the lame excuse that he had only a son. Should that insult not be expunged in blood? The Trojan War, he felt, had been ignited for more frivolous reasons. What was the honor of Menelaus compared to the extinction of the des Tilleuls family line?[62]

---

58. "I leave you."

59. *Quos ego*: Beginning of line 135 of Book I of Virgil's *Aeneid*: "You whom I should…"

60. "How long." *Quo usque tandem abutere, Catilina, patientia nostra* is a Latin phrase from Marcus Tullius Cicero's first speech against Catiline. It means "How long, Catiline, will you abuse our patience?" These words constitute the famous Incipit, which is the beginning of the first speech against Catiline. This speech was given by Cicero in the Temple of Jupiter Stator (the speech was not held in the Roman Senate for security reasons) on the eighth of November in 63 B.C. in order to uncover and punish the second Catilinarian conspiracy, an attempted coup by Catiline and his supporters against the Roman Republic.

61. "But in fact." Another quote from Cicero, from paragraph 194 of Book III of the Second Speech to impeach Verres, one of Catiline's friends. Gaius Verres (ca. 120 – 43 B.C.) was a Roman magistrate, notorious for his misgovernment of Sicily. Extortion was the process by which the governors of Roman provinces could be called to account by their oppressed subjects. The most notorious case is that of Catiline's friend Verres. Verres returned to Rome in 70 B.C., and in the same year, at the request of the Sicilians, Marcus Tullius Cicero prosecuted him.

62. In Greek mythology, Menelaus (ancient Greek: Μενέλαος) was a legendary king of Mycenaean Sparta. His wife Helen was abducted by the Trojan prince Paris,

As the unrecognizable professor continued on his way, tacking back and forth, he bumped into a body of considerable bulk.

"*Cave ne cadas*," he said. [63]

"*Cave ne cadas*," was the reply.

It seemed to the pious Paraclet that he had encountered a rock with an echo.

"Who are you?" he asked.

"Monsieur Paraclet," said a human voice, "I am the court clerk. My hair is white. Please listen to me."

"The court has made its decision," said Naso, in his most ironic voice. "You have come to read me my death sentence."

"Monsieur," said the clerk, "I sign my ministry's documents with my name, Maro Lafourchette, and I am indeed your humble servant." [64]

"Then serve me by being a target for the arrows of my wrath."

"Monsieur, listen to me."

"You, a simple clerk, an innocent pen-pusher, an obscure paper-shuffler, you bump into a man like me as he walks along, deep in thought."

"But after all…"

"Run along, you miserable creature!"

"But…"

"Run along, you nitpicking bourgeois!"

"Do not insult the unfortunate," said the clerk. "*Ne insultes miseris*."

"Or, *ne insulta*," replied Naso,

"Or, *noli insultare miseris*" countered the worthy Lafourchette. [65]

---

an incident that led to the Trojan War. He was the son of Atreus and Aerope, and brother of Agamemnon king of Mycenae and leader of the Greek army during the war. Prominent in both the *Iliad* and *Odyssey*, Menelaus was also popular in Greek vase painting and Greek tragedy.

63. "Be careful not to fall" (Lhomond's Grammar, page 205).

64. In French, *la fourchette* is the fork. Usually, in Verne's works, proper names have a double meaning. Very often, the name says something about the role the character plays in the narration – Nemo (Latin for no one) in *Vingt mille lieues sous les mers* (*Twenty Thousand Leagues Under the Seas*, 1869) is a typical example.

65. Verne copied all three verbal forms from Lhomond's Grammar, page 175.

The professor's anger was instantly assuaged by these grammatical quotations. He had found a Latin scholar of his own caliber.

"What does the honorable clerk want of me?" he asked.

"I overheard your conversation with Monsieur de Pertinax. Please forgive my unintentional indiscretion. I can be of some service to you."

The clever clerk was using the two-sided key of insinuation to open the door of the professor's intellect.

"My name is Maro, as in Virgil,[66] he said.

"And Lafourchette, like nobody else," replied Naso. "What of it?"

"I am the father of a nubile daughter of some means. "She is, in the fullest sense of the word, what Justinian calls *viropotens*." [67]

"*Viropotens*?" asked Naso.

"*Viropotens*," repeated Maro.

The professor was touched. "Monsieur," he said, "that *viropotens* makes me your friend for life. And what is the name of this *viropotens* daughter?"

"Eglantine. A woman of gentle ways, a pleasant companion, well-connected socially, free of debt, and with an iron constitution. Marriage would appropriately satisfy her youthful impatience, if Monsieur le Marquis des Tilleuls would deign to let his majestic eyes fall on her and do us the honor of spending the evening of this happy day at our home.

"Now there is a fine sentence," said Naso, beginning to ponder the matter. The future of the des Tilleuls dynasty was in his hands!

"*Quota hora est*?" he asked.[68]

"*Quinta*," replied Lafourchette.[69]

"At seven o'clock, Monsieur le Marquis and I will knock on your door."

---

66. The poet's full name was Publius Vergilius Maro.

67. Flavius Petrus Sabbatius Iustinianus (483 – 565) is known in English as Justinian I or Justinian the Great. He was the second member of the Justinian Dynasty (after his uncle, Justin I) and Eastern Roman Emperor from 527 until his death. He is considered a saint amongst Eastern Orthodox Christians, and is also commemorated by some Lutheran churches. *Viripotens*: A legal term meaning "marriageable." Verne was a lawyer, having passed what would be today the bar examination in 1850.

68. "What time is it?" (Lhomond's Grammar, page 173).

69. "Five o'clock," literally "the fifth (hour)."

Thereupon, those illustrious persons concluded the duet of their scientific eloquence and Paraclet, deep in thought, wended his way back to the castle.

What a mismatch! The daughter of a provincial court clerk grafting herself onto a haughty des Tilleuls! This ancient tree would shake its white flowers down upon prosaic heads. Far from the estates cultivated by his ancestors, he would find himself transported to the fields of the bourgeoisie, made up of bits of land pieced together.

But there was little choice in the matter. The family would be revived and its descendants would confer its glory on every succeeding generation. And besides, Anselme would enhance his wife's status, as the rooster confers nobility on the hen.

Reassured by this barn-yard line of reasoning, the professor soon reached the castle and announced to the young marquis that he had achieved complete success. Repressing his extramarital fervor, he gave him a lecture, Ciceronian in length and argumentation, on the purpose of legitimate unions, considered from the standpoint both of morality and of procreation.

On hearing the silvery name of Lafourchette, Anselme did not frown. With his innocent disposition, he gave it only perfunctory consideration and left it at that. Eglantine was a woman; what more did he need? He was still at that naïve and happy age at which one is ready to marry any dress, even a dressing gown.

After dinner, with great excitement, the castle proceeded to deck the young marquis out in all his finery. His people were busy for two hours. Cascades of purifying water poured down over his ingenuous forehead until the towels thought they were losing their white fabric. Jars of ointment were emptied of their sweet-smelling contents. Combs were broken and replaced among the virgin forests that crowned the young marquis's head. Boot-hooks strained as they struggled with stubborn boots. Armoires disgorged floods of clothing. Suspenders wore out their elastic to attain a pressure of several atmospheres. An endless array of cravats unrolled in all directions their alligator wrinkles.

At the appointed time, the marquis looked like a bear wearing cuffs, a lace shirt-front, and a ceremonial sword.

In a few minutes, accompanied by his stiff and starched professor, he arrived at no. 7, Vieux-Parchemin Street, and prepared to make his triumphant entry.

Everyone was there. Monsieur Lafourchette and his daughter Eglantine; their cousin Boussigneau, the deputy mayor; the Grognons, distant relatives of the Lafourchettes and everyone else; the young lady's godfather, one Protêt, an official bailiff with a law degree. [70]

The salon gleamed in the light of two candles shining sadly at each end. Hideous portraits of the perfect hunter hung piteously in the four corners, while a ridiculous mahogany table, bearing a cage of stuffed birds, played the role of the fifth partner. Chairs and upholstered armchairs offered their questionable softness to the visitors. Only the sergeant of the mounted police could sit on them for an hour at a time, and that was because his calling had made the fleshy parts of his body as hard as wood. A piano, which seemed out of place in front of the window, and which must have held within it the faithful echo of the kitchen pots and pans, completed the picture.

The Marquis des Tilleuls was announced. Panic set in among the guests, but they quickly recovered. Anselme made his appearance under the crossfire of nervous stares. The men got to their feet, the women curtsied, and the children looked closely to see whether the stranger had wires attached to his arms and legs to make him move.

Naso formally introduced his pupil and Eglantine walked toward him under cover of the all-engulfing and auspicious darkness. When she greeted him, her forty-five years joined in the greeting. She was, in fact, flourishing in the sunny summertime and the Indian summer of life. Eglantine was large, short, corpulent, squat, round, and spherical. She wore her own hair and displayed a wide variety of ornaments in the shape of tropical plants.

To Anselme's eyes she was magnificent, a larger-than-life version of Venus Aphrodite; and so she might have seemed, through the prism of youthful passion. [71] She might easily have been mistaken for her own mother, although she was only the daughter.

In short, they greeted each other, exchanged compliments, sat

---

70. *Grognon* in French means grumbling, peevish. Used by Verne as a family name makes it even more sarcastic.

71. In the manuscript, Verne writes Aphrodite with a lowercase "a," which means that he considers it as an adjective. Aphrodite is the Greek goddess of love and beauty, and Venus the Roman goddess of beauty and love. After the conquest of Ancient Greece by Rome, the two divinities were merged and considered as one goddess. The same process of identification is true for Zeus and Jupiter, Hades and Pluto, Hera and Juno, etc.

down, and chatted. The conversation turned from the general to the particular. Seated next to the clerk's daughter, the marquis spoke so softly that they might have been saying nothing at all to each other.

Naso spoke Latin with his new friend, whose style he found reminiscent of Quintilian, and revealed to him his latest observations about irregular declensions. [72]

They played *corbillon*. [73] Although this game had been explained to the marquis a hundred times, his rebellious intelligence could not fathom its euphonic character, and the heterogeneous endings he uttered came as a painful surprise to the assembled guests.

As for the good professor, he invariably put in the name of his friend Lhomond.

The rest of the guests were becoming accustomed to the sight of the young marquis, with his physical and mental imperfections.

But the engaged couple (for they were now plighted to one another by their love) were intoxicated with happiness. Soon Anselme became excited, talked about the irregular noun *cubile* and taught his beloved the declension of *tonitru*. [74] She had apparently known how to decline *cornu*, horn, since birth. Eglantine answered him with "fat woman," "expedition," and "assize court." [75]

Then, for the sake of variety, they played a few harmless games. At blind man's bluff, Anselme got the sexes strangely confused and soon upset the table and the bird cage. If only the birds could have come to life, they would have flown away. In the game of synonyms, he was told that the object he was supposed to guess was good, virtuous, and sensitive, that it was a source of delight, a subject of study, and the sweetest of pastimes, that it was kept next to one's heart, under one's pillow, and in one's prayer book. His answer was "a windmill."

---

72. Marcus Fabius Quintilianus (ca. 35 – ca. 100) was a Roman rhetorician from northern Hispania (today Spain), widely referred to in medieval schools of rhetoric and in Renaissance writing.

73. In this game, one player says to another "What will you put in my little basket (*corbillon*)?" The other player must reply with a noun that rhymes with *corbillon*. It is mentioned by Molière in *The School of Women* (act I, scene I, line 3).

74. *Cubile*: "Bed" (Lhomond's Grammar, page 102). *Tonitru*: "Thunder" (Lhomond's Grammar, page 9).

75. *Cornu*: Lhomond's Grammar, page 8, where it is presented as example of the fourth declension.

The evening finally came to an end on a favorable note. The young marquis thought he saw Eglantine in his dreams, and she fantasized about the innocent delights of a spotless husband.

The next day the marriage was arranged, and a week later the church bells rang out a thousand flattering promises to the ears of the prospective bride and groom.

Naso Paraclet kept hopping about on one foot all day long. He was no longer recognizable. His wishes were about to be fulfilled, and he could see his dear pupil's descendants planting long lines of des Tilleuls.

The great day arrived, but for some reason the Mirabelles, the Vieille Pierres, and the Pertinaxes did not die of vexation.

The marquis was blushing like a vestal virgin in broad daylight. He had lighted the sacred flame of marriage and kept it burning with religious care. His Latin studies had suffered slightly from a quite pardonable lack of attention, but once the knot was tied it would be actively resumed, and young Anselme was planning to translate word for word the passionate love between Dido and Aeneas.

O good and innocent young man, run to where happiness awaits you, where pleasures beckon. Open your bosom to the powerful embraces of a corpulent wife. Hold in your outstretched arms the two hundred and fifty pounds of living flesh placed there by love. Let your intelligence be caressed by the poetic inspiration of the God of Cythera and untie, with a lawful hand, the maidenly girdle of your languorous fiancée.

The pious professor took his pupil aside, instructed him in his conjugal duties, and gave him a beautiful paraphrase of the scriptural *duo in una carne*.[76] Leafing endlessly through the great book of the world's mysteries, the Marquis des Tilleuls found the supreme teachings in its creative pages.

Then the professor and the pupil went on to the practical deductions of life. Anselme was forewarned about inappropriate advances by amorous intruders. He felt his forehead go pale and his hair stand on end on hearing of the errors that might be committed by the weaker sex. He was terrified as he read the biographies of famous husbands of ancient times and contemplated, beneath the world's troubled waters, shoals whose existence he had never suspected. Life,

---

76. "Two persons in one flesh."

like the sea, seemed to him to have smooth, sandy banks. Then he cast the sounding line and found a rocky bottom that had shattered many matrimonial hulls and would shatter many more.

But Naso raised his downcast spirits. Fortune was with him in the alliance he was about to contract. Eglantine Lafourchette seemed ideally suited to make a husband happy. She would be impervious to various attempts at seduction and would escape anti-marital attempts on her virtue. She was a carefully cultivated field, and out of her love for Anselme she was creating a scarecrow to put voracious birds and destructive suitors to flight.

The marquis's marriage was now simply a melodious theme without variations, accidentals, or coda, composed in the key of pleasure and happiness.

The wedding evening was moving and passionate. The impatient marquis wanted to retire before sunset, but the energetic professor, always the stalwart friend of convention, held him back with an ablative absolute and an absolute will-power, which he could not disobey.

"Delay, my noble pupil, delay the mysterious moment when the future of your passions will blend with the present of exquisite delight. And do not forget the different ways of expressing the preposition 'without' before an infinitive. You can spend the night without sleeping (*noctem insomnem ducere*), without harming your conscience (*salva fide*), without pretending to take no notice (*dissimulanter*).[77] Remember that marriage is nothing but a translation and that you must translate your wife word for word before attempting too free a version."

At last the star of Venus rose above the horizon of pleasure. Anselme's impatient telescope had already been trained on it long since.[78]

The lovely Eglantine Lafourchette tried in vain to weep. Her modesty had not been able to swell the rivulet of her tears. Her eyes did not overflow. She rolled her immense and gently agitated form toward the conjugal bedroom, and the guests, seeming, in spirit at least, to be somewhere else, filed past the marquis.

---

77. The three examples of Latin language in the sentence are taken from Lhomond's Grammar, page 266, in the chapter "How to use the preposition *without* before an infinitive."

78. The combination of the words "Venus" and "telescope" is a scatological double-entendre typical of Verne.

Naso's paternal eyelashes were wet with unbidden tears, and his friend Maro could only express himself by exclaiming *O, evax, hei, papœ, hui!*[79]

At last Anselme des Tilleuls, until then the last of that name, kissed his professor and his father-in-law, and slipped away.

The birds fluttered in their nests of greenery. In the fragrant breath of the wind, night silently ruffled the diaphanous curtains of its ebony bed. The evening star looked down with its rays through the mysterious darkness, and heaven, adding its provocative echoes to the muffled sighs, quivered for a moment with pleasure, youth, and love.

Nine months later, the des Tilleuls were in full bloom and nothing troubled the domestic happiness of the united families. Only father-in-law Lafourchette, who, like all old court clerks, was a bit of a tease, challenged Naso on the difficulties of scientific Latin.

"Are you familiar with Phaedrus?[80] The clerk asked him.

"Of course!"

"How would you translate *anus ad amphoram*?[81]

"*Anus*, "the old woman," *ad amphoram*, "to the amphora." It's the title of a fable.

"You are making a gross error."

"Indeed!" said the worthy Paraclet.

"A disgusting error!"

"Monsieur Maro, be careful what you say."

"*Amphoram* is translated as 'pot.'"

"What does that matter?"

"*Ad* means 'on.'"

"Well then?"

"And *anus* does not mean 'old woman.'"[82]

---

79. Interjections expressing admiration, according to Lhomond's Grammar, page 97.

80. Phaedrus (ca. 15 B.C. – ca. A.D. 50), Roman fabulist, was probably a Thracian slave, born in Pydna of Macedonia (Roman province) and lived in the reigns of Augustus, Tiberius, Caligula and Claudius. He is recognized as the first writer to Latinize entire books of fables, retelling in iambic Latin verse the Greek prose of Aesop's fables.

81. *Anus ad amphoram* ("The Old Woman and Empty Cask") is the title of the first fable of the third book of Aesop's fables written by Phaedrus.

82. Again, a direct use of scatological humor by Verne.

A virtuous fury shot through Paraclet, and the two champions would have started to tear each other's hair out if they had not been separated—and wearing wigs.

Soon even those incidents came to an end, and the two champions provoked no more mental riots. They left the dagger of jest and the fire-tongs of sarcasm to rust in one corner of their minds.

The fact is that life was tranquil in that favorite city, where the paving stones enjoyed uninterrupted repose.

The Marquis des Tilleuls saw no cloud on the horizon of his happiness. Children, male or female as the case might be, arrived every year to consolidate the hope of an eternal posterity, and the pious Naso Paraclet, having concluded his remarks on irregular declensions, spent his time researching the secret causes which, in both the grammatical and the marital sense, prevent intransitive verbs from governing the accusative case.

○

The Tribulations of a Translator of Jules Verne

by Edward Baxter

Reading a work of fiction is more than an intellectual exercise of deriving ideas from the printed word. It is above all an emotional experience, which makes the reader laugh and weep, shudder and cringe, while sharing the joys, fears, anticipation, and anger of the fictional characters.

But for that to happen the writer and reader must find a common language, hence the need for the translator, whose task is to give the reader, in his or her mother tongue, not only the factual information contained in the original text, but also the emotional experience offered to the writer's original audience. Although a translation can never hope to equal the original in literary merit, most readers would agree that an imperfect translation is better than none at all, as witness the millions of copies of translated books in libraries and bookstores. According to an article published in the Swiss newsweekly *Hebdo* in May, 1989, the three most widely translated literary works in the world are, in order, the Bible, the writings of V.I. Lenin, and the novels of Jules Verne.

Some of the difficulties encountered by the translator of Verne are no different from those that must be surmounted in translating a novel by any other French writer. There is, first of all, the need to be thoroughly familiar with the subject matter of the work in hand, for this is often essential to finding the most appropriate English equivalent for a French word or expression. *Le pays des fourrures* (*The Fur Country*, 1873), for example, opens with a party at a Hudson's Bay Company trading post in the Canadian far north. One of the dishes being served to the guests is something called, in French, "boeuf musqué," which, in an early English version, was translated as "musk beef." The reader may well have wondered what kind of exotic Arctic delicacy the guests were being treated to. Had the translator been as well-informed about Arctic flora and fauna as Verne was, however, he would have found the word he needed—"muskox."

Then there is the question of finding the right level of language, not only for the narration, but also for each character, in order to reflect their distinct personalities. The reader of *Famille-sans-nom* (*Family Without a Name*, 1889) who did not notice a difference between the speech of the garrulous, jocular Master Nick and the carefully measured words of the serious and fearless Jean Sans-nom would have missed something that the author intended his readers to enjoy.

In *Family Without a Name*, also, there is a marked difference in style between the chapters that are mainly historical and those in which Verne's own fictional characters play the leading role. The actual historical figures who appear in the book come across as very stereotyped characters, in contrast to the Huron notary, Nick Sagamore, or the farmer Jean Harcher and his wife. (There must be some significance to the fact that the historical characters and the fictional characters never meet face to face.) Whether the aim of making the historical sections sound as interesting as the fictional parts can really be achieved is open to question. The translator's reach must exceed his grasp.

Each language, too, has its own stylistic preferences. The passive voice is much commoner in English than in French, while French shows a fondness for relative clauses that in English are more likely to appear as principal clauses or even separate sentences. If such differences are not taken into account, the reader of the translation will have the impression of listening to a well-educated Frenchman speaking English.

All this holds true whether one is translating Jules Verne or any other French novelist. But Verne did have his own idiosyncrasies of style, which present a particular challenge to the translator.

Perhaps it was his own early attempts at writing verse that gave Verne his penchant for introducing poetry into his novels. In *The Fur Country*, for instance, the Inuit girl Kalumah sings a folk song of her people that begins with the following stanza:

Le ciel est noir
Et le soleil se traîne
À peine!
De désespoir
Ma pauvre âme incertaine
Est pleine!
La blonde enfant se rit de mes tendres chansons,
Et sur son coeur l'hiver promène ses glaçons!

What the translator has to convey here is not simply the meaning of the words, which could be done most accurately in prose, but the feel of rhyme and rhythm, and the theme of unrequited love in the frozen north. It may well be true that poetry is "what gets lost in the translation," but readers have been told they are going to have a song, and a song they must have. Here is one attempt:

Dark is the sky,
The brief course of the sun
Is done,
And sad am I.
When shall my troubled breast
Find rest?
The fair-haired maiden laughs at my imploring songs.
Colder than ice is she for whom my spirit longs.

A similar challenge confronts the translator in *Family Without a Name*, where Lionel Restigouche, a junior clerk in the office of Master Nick Sagamore, a Huron notary, decides to enter a poetry contest sponsored by the League of Poets. He gives his entry the romantic title of *Le Feu follet* (*Will-o'-the-wisp*). Here are the two opening stanzas:

Ce feu fantasque, insaisissable,
Qui, le soir, se dégage et luit,
Et qui, dans l'ombre de la nuit,
Ni sur la mer ni sur le sable,
Ne laisse de trace après lui!

Ce feu toujours prêt à s'éteindre,
Tantôt blanchâtre ou violet,
Pour reconnaître ce qu'il est,
Il faudrait le pouvoir atteindre…
Atteignez donc un feu follet!

Here again, the only acceptable translation is one that gives the English reader the emotional experience of reading verse. Prose, however faithful to the original in meaning, will not do if it is supposed to impress the League of Poets, and the translator has no choice but to try to capture some of the exaggerated romanticism of Lionel's literary effort, in approximately the same meter and rhyme-scheme.

This weird, elusive, dancing flame,
Which seems at eventide to shine,
And which, at night, appears to stand
Upon the sea, or on the sand,
While leaving not a trace behind,

This ever-nearly-dying flame,
Whitish, or tinged with violet,
How can we know it? We must strive
To capture it, alight, alive.
Will-o'-the-wisp, I'll have you yet!

More than any other literary device, the pun is the bane of the translator's existence. By definition, it defies translation, for it consists of using words that are nearly alike in sound, but different in meaning. Jules Verne was not by any means the only French novelist to indulge in puns, but he did make them a regular part of his stock-in-trade.

When young Lionel Restigouche attempts to justify his own versifying by invoking the names of such distinguished French-Canadian poets as Octave Crémazie, William Chapman, and Pamphile Lemay, his employer retorts that these gentlemen "ne sont pas payés six piastres par mois—et par moi!" for copying legal documents. To have Master Nick say that they "are not paid six dollars a month—and by me!" conveys the meaning, but misses the joke. It might have been possible in this case to transfer the pun to another word ("they are not paid six dollars a month in hard cash—my hard-earned cash"), but usually the result is so contrived that it is better to leave out the pun altogether (even at the cost of having to delete Verne's comment that Nick was "delighted with his own play on words.")

English writers who give their novels a French setting often refer to certain characters as "monsieur," "madame," and "mademoiselle," as a way of introducing local color into their writing. The words are perfectly familiar to English readers, and help to keep their minds focused on the locale. The same thing occurs, in reverse, in *The Fur Country*, where over and over again, (sometimes more than once on a single page), the heroine is referred to as "Mrs. Paulina Barnett." As a device for keeping before the French reader the fact that this woman who speaks such polished French is in fact English, it is effective, but there is no need for it in the English translation. The effect is not local color, but boredom, certainly not what the author intended. To avoid introducing into the English version a negative element that was not part of the original French, the translator has to use more variety in referring to Verne's heroine. She can be "Mrs. Barnett," "Paulina," or simply "she."

One of the alternative words Verne himself uses in referring to Mrs. Paulina Barnett (after all, even as local color, it can be overdone!) is *la voyageuse*. This presents a new problem. English does not have different words for male and female travelers, and the word "traveler" could refer to any of the twenty-odd members of the Hudson's Bay Company expedition who make up the cast of characters. Such turns of phrase as "the lady traveler" or "the traveling woman" are at best awkward and at worst sexist. The only solution here is to recognize that the author is using the word simply to prevent repetition from getting out of hand, and translate it by a proper noun or a pronoun.

It is probably also to lend an exotic flavor to *The Fur Country* that Verne gives all temperature readings in Fahrenheit. Then, for the benefit of his French readers, he gives the Centigrade equivalent in parentheses. For most English readers, there is nothing exotic at all about Fahrenheit thermometers, and the parenthetical explanation becomes a distraction which is better left out altogether. (Perhaps, as the metric system spreads throughout the English-speaking world, the conversions to Centigrade will have to be put back in.)

Although Verne's novels show evidence of careful research, they sometimes contain surprising inaccuracies. In the case of such minor errors as a misspelled name or an incorrect date, there seems to be no point in perpetuating them. Hence, for example, the poet referred to as "Chapemann" in *Family Without a Name* resumes his true name of Chapman, and when the British astronomer Thomas Black, in *The Fur Country*, calculates the interval between 1860 and 1896 as "vingt-six ans," it appears in translation as "thirty-six years." One can only hope that Verne would have approved these editorial corrections, had they been made during his lifetime.

There are other mistakes of a different order. For instance, in *Family Without a Name*, the *Patriotes* of Lower Canada (Quebec) make their last stand on Navy Island, in the Niagara River. In fact, it was the English-speaking rebels from Upper Canada (Ontario) who occupied Navy Island. In a history text, this would be a serious error, but the writer of historical fiction is allowed to take certain liberties. In any case, to attempt to correct this kind of mistake would damage the novel more than it would improve it, and the most that the translator should undertake is to draw attention to it in an introduction.

There is often a temptation to edit or shorten geographical data, especially in cases where it is not essential to the plot. On the whole, it seems better not to tamper with anything that has been put into the mouths of the characters in the novel. It would be anachronistic to have them talking about Oslo when it was still Christiania, or Alaska, when everyone else was calling it Russian America. Besides, it gives a touch of local color to use place-names that have now been changed. They could be explained in a foot-note, but it is probably better to assume that the reader will either know what places are being referred to, not care what the modern names are anyway, or look them up in an encyclopedia.

The use of the word *Esquimau* in *The Fur Country* presented a particular problem, because it is a term that is offensive to the northern native peoples to whom it is applied. It would have been straining credibility to have the characters in the story use the term *Inuit*, which was almost unknown to English speakers of the time, but there is a case for using it in the narrative part of the novel, on the grounds that it is an accurate translation of *Esquimau*, and that it is the term Verne himself would have used if he were writing today.

Verne did a great deal of research for his novels and sometimes he succumbed to the temptation to incorporate great masses of statistics into them. In chapter 10 of *The Fur Country*, for instance, Captain

Craventy gives Paulina Barnett a five-page history of the Hudson's Bay Company. This was probably more interesting to readers in Verne's own day, before any white explorer had reached the North Pole, than to us who live in an age when anyone with enough money can take a 24-hour flight over the Pole and be back at work on Monday morning. Artistically, little would be lost if this historical data were omitted or abbreviated, but the insight it gives into the characters of Captain Craventy and Paulina Barnett justifies leaving it intact. Readers know they are not studying a history text, and if they find the statistics too boring, they can simply skim over them.

The "Extraordinary Journeys" will always appeal to readers who are fascinated by exotic places, by innovative technology, and by the struggle of oppressed peoples for freedom, and translators will always continue their efforts to do justice to the work of a writer who has been described as "the man who invented the future."

◯

Appendix:

Jédédias Jamet,
or The Tale of an Inheritance

An unfinished novel by Jules Verne

**Translated and with a Preface and
Annotations by Kieran M. O'Driscoll**

The following is a first translation into English of three chapters written by Jules Verne, most probably while he was still only in his late teens or early twenties. The fact that Verne originally intended this work to become a complete novel before abandoning it is attested to by the rough draft outline which he produced of the projected entire story, a summary which has also been here rendered into English.

These chapters were written, it seems, during a period when Jules was, at his father's behest, studying law in Paris with a view to eventually inheriting the family law practice in Nantes. However, the young man's true ambitions lay not in the legal, but rather the literary domain. His less than willing immersion in the legal world probably explains one of the principal themes, which deals with questions of succession and inheritance, and offers a satirical portrait of the legal profession and of its sometimes greedy clients.

The central character, Monsieur Jédédias Jamet, is a pillar of the small community within which he resides, the town of Chinon in the Touraine region of France. Though he is a good father, husband, juror and member of the National Guard, he is depicted with supreme irony by Verne as an inept individual who lives in blissful ignorance of his own incompetence. For instance, his wildly erroneous predictions and instructions lead to the destruction by fire of several farms, the drowning of an unfortunate dog, the failure of numerous harvests, the killing of many hunters, and the loss of much livestock.

Notwithstanding, he is revered by the locals; and so the general populace equally becomes a target of Verne's ridicule. Thus, after allowing a wretched canine to drown—yet cannily turning the error to his own advantage—does Jamet become "the oracle of the locality," using his "rightfully acquired fame" to dispense "excellent advice."

Jamet is obsessed with neatness. He jealously guards, and preserves in mint condition, the coat he has inherited from his late father, his "minimum legal entitlement," a "mediocre legacy." Anything else that he might have acquired from the paternal estate has been cruelly denied him by the greed of others, and Jamet appears as a rather pathetic figure.

On the other hand, Jamet considers that this is "the coat to which he owe[s] his happiness," in that he feels it helped him to win the heart of his spouse, Perpetua Tertullien. However, Verne, again satirizing human greed, hints strongly that Perpetua's family, in reality, consented to the marriage thanks to her suitor having become rich as a result of an inheritance from a cousin.

Jamet's mathematical exactness in relation to his coat seems reminiscent of the obsessive-compulsive precision of that subsequent and much more famous Vernian automaton, Phileas Fogg, in *Le Tour du monde en quatre-vingts jours* (*Around the World in Eighty Days*, 1873). Thus does Jamet "attire…himself in his coat, in accordance with the rules of applied geometry of the thumb and index finger" and, with a flick of his fingers, he rids the garment of "those microcosmic specks which he alone could discern."

The heavily guarded coat is likened to a virginal daughter whose chasteness is jealously guarded by a vigilant mother ("a dread-afflicted mother [who] keeps her daughter captive under her wing"). Nobody must place a "defiling hand" on the "spotless" garment. Jamet constantly fears for "the virginal luster of his vestments," and lives "in dread of any base or obscene fondling of the sole object of his thoughts." This, as we shall see, is one of several sexual subtexts and uses of sexualized language, permeating the story.

The tale begins as Jamet receives a mysterious note advising him of the death of an uncle of his wife, viz. M. Opime Romauld Tertullien. This is a most unusual "death notice" in that it is apparently written by the deceased himself, and fails to give the sender's address, or the location of the bizarrely-named Church of Saint Collette the Hip Swayer, in which the memorial service is to take place. Following this cryptic communication, the narrator pauses to describe Jamet's life and to offer flashbacks to significant previous events in his life, before recounting the consequences of the "mysterious parchment" received by Jamet.

The notice causes Jamet to rush to the home of his solicitor in a state of feverish anticipation of a possible large inheritance, tempered by his fear that other relatives and claimants may deprive him of his hypothetical bequest. Jamet's long and frenzied monologue to his solicitor (who listens to him while freezing in the cold water of his morning bath) strongly satirizes mercenary natures; the greed, perhaps, of some of the potential heirs whom Verne probably encountered in his legal work. Perpetua, too, sheds brief crocodile tears for her late uncle but is much more concerned with inheriting the wealth of this successful businessman.

It seems, from Verne's draft, that the remainder of this unfinished work would have recounted the tale of Jamet's fruitless international journey in pursuit of the supposed inheritance. The journey would have been strewn with increasing mystery, obstacles and frustrations, and the story in its entirety would, it seems, have been as bizarre as its first three chapters.

There are, in fact, three inheritances referred to in this *Tale of an Inheritance*. Apart from the potential inheritance from Perpetua's late uncle, there is the much cared-for coat which Jamet has acquired from his father, and there is also the inheritance which contributed to Jamet's winning the approval of Perpetua's family, viz. Jamet had become "wealthy as a result of an inheritance from one of his cousins, an intrepid aviator who had dropped himself from a height of three thousand meters."

This short text is peppered with references of a legal, historical, religious and mythological nature which combine to give this ironic text a mock "learned" air. Annotations have been provided, thus fulfilling the didactic duty of the translator. Legal references in this story include allusions to particular kinds of bailiffs, to succession law, to court orders for the seizure of debtors' possessions, and to secured and unsecured loans. Religious and Biblical references include those to Saint Colette, the Seven Deadly Sins, the story of Joseph in the Old Testament's Book of Genesis, the priest Urbain Grandier, the character Holopherne in the Old Testament's Book of Judith, and the Old Testament story of the Ten Plagues of Egypt. Mythological references are abundant, so that Verne grandiosely links characters and events in his text to such figures as Horace, Augustus, Plato and Diogenes, and to the walls of Carthage and the siege of Troy. Historical and literary references are to such persons as Henri II of Navarre, César Vichard de Saint-Réal and the writers Berquin and Molière.

As the names which Verne chooses for his characters in other, later stories sometimes appear to hint, however obliquely, at personal traits (e.g. Fogg, Passepartout, Fix, Nemo, Conseil or Captain Speedy), what might be the significance of the name Jédédias Jamet chosen by Verne for this central character? The English equivalent of Jédédias is Jedediah; and Jedediah Smith (1799 – c.1831) was a hunter, explorer and fur trader operating in the Rocky Mountains, the Southwest, and the West coast of the United States. Might Verne, through his overriding interest in literary themes of exploration and his later setting of some novels in the United States, have been aware of this explorer? As for the surname Jamet, there was a French priest called Denis Jamet or Jamay (died 1625) who was the first superior of the Canadian mission of his Recollect order of priests. "Jamay" is also the name of a town in Mexico. "Jamet" is also a homophone of the French word "jamais" ("never"). These are merely a number of speculative possibilities.

Finally—and as alluded to earlier in this Preface—there are some bizarre scatological, and specifically sexual, elements scattered throughout these chapters. For instance, Verne hints that Jamet's marriage is now sexless, but that there was a time when Perpetua "would vouch for the fact that [Jamet] was never rushed under any circumstances." There are two references to excretion; Jamet's son is suffering from indigestion, and the family cat suffers from constipation. This is, in many ways, a bizarre, surreal text, which seems, superficially at least, to bear little resemblance to the themes of Verne's later works.

On closer inspection, however, it can be seen that *Jédédias Jamet, or The Tale of an Inheritance,* would, if completed, have dealt with the quintessential Vernian trope of a long journey of exploration and discovery through different countries (including the United States), undertaken by the central character in the company of a trusted valet. Furthermore, even these early chapters already contain themes which seem to "haunt" Verne's later, celebrated works: Jamet's obsessive-compulsive, unhurried behavior and his preoccupation with mathematical exactness suggest an early model for Phileas Fogg. Although Fogg would hardly have shown the excessive excitement manifested by Jamet when he receives news of his wife's uncle's death, there may be similar undertones in that novel. This unfinished Verne work deserves attention, as it offers some insight into the mind of the early writer.

Chapter I

Which treats of Monsieur Jededias Jamet, his physical appearance, his state of mind, his coat, his waistcoat and his trousers

> To Monsieur Jamet,
> Property owner, Tours, France.

> Dear Sir,

> Monsieur Opime Romauld Tertullien, former merchant, member of the Legion of Honor and of several other learned associations, most regretfully notifies you of the loss, which he has recently suffered, of his own person, viz. the above-named Opime Jédédias Tertullien. He most respectfully requests you to attend the funeral service which will take place, for the repose of his soul, at the Church of Saint Collette the Hip Swayer.[1]

> 13th June, 1842.

---

1. Saint Colette de Corbie (1381–1447), born Nicolette Boylet or Boellet, was the founder of the order of Colettine Poor Clares (the Clarisses), a reformation of the Urbanist Poor Clares. For the convents which she later reformed, she prescribed extreme poverty, to go barefooted, and the observance of perpetual fast and abstinence. Why Verne jokingly describes her here as "déhanchée" ("standing with one's weight on one hip/lopsided/waddling/hip-swaying") is unclear.

Monsieur Jamet was a property owner and a native of the Touraine region of France; just like the snail, he had never come out of his shell.[2] The more malicious residents of the town of Chinon, situated nine leagues from Tours, swore upon oath that they had seen his horns! But the inhabitants of the Vairon region are generally considered to be rather spiteful scandalmongers, similar to the denizens of Nantes and of Evroite.

Whatever the case may be, Monsieur Jédédias Jamet allowed these malicious tongue-waggers to carry on with their offensive remarks, and was not at all diminished in the pride with which he gave his arm to Madame Perpetua Jamet, née Romauld Tertullien.

Their union had produced young Francis, and the beautiful Joséphine; Monsieur Jamet having promised that he would leave it at that, Madame Perptua lived in perpetual adoration of the Lord and of his representatives here on Earth.

M. Jamet was not the jealous type; indeed, he could never have been accused of either pride, lust, gluttony, sloth, wrath, greed, or envy![3] He had never killed anybody, nor had he ever permitted himself to commit the slightest error in his private depositions. Besides, he was a fine member of the National Guard,[4] a juror who was always alert and on standby, a tender and docile husband, a sensible and peaceable voter and a man whose company was always most agreeable, so that his reputation for possessing a high degree of integrity—an integrity which had not been tarnished by the century's corruption—had spread as far as Loudun.

---

2.   The Touraine is a former province of France. Its capital was Tours. Traversed by the Loire and its tributaries, the Cher, the Indre and the Vienne, it makes up a part of the Paris Basin, and is well known for its viticulture.

3.   These are the Seven Deadly Sins, also known as the Capital Vices, or Cardinal Sins, within the teaching of the Catholic Church.

4.   The National Guard (French: la Garde nationale) was the name given at the time of the French Revolution to the militias formed in each city, on the model of the National Guard established in Paris. Having been dissolved by Charles X in 1827, a new National Guard was set up in 1831 following the July Revolution of 1830, under the leadership of the Republican Marquis de Lafayette. It fought in the Revolution of 1848, but was later confined by Napoleon III, during the Second Empire, to subordinate tasks in order to reduce its liberal and Republican influence.

An optimist by nature, he did not believe stories of the alleged cruelty of the notorious Duke of Albret,[5] and his smooth, beardless cheeks would be masked with a white, virginal color, whenever anybody spoke to him of Joseph's 'coat of many colors'[6], or of the bewitchment of the Ursuline nuns by the priest Urbain Grandier:[7]

"Urbain did not at all expose those Daughters of the Lord to the Devil," he would add, with the air of an enraptured novice, "and the only reason that the Pharaoh's wife modestly snatched the clothing of Jacob's son out of his hands, was in order to veil the early-morning disarray of her own dress."[8]

Monsieur Jamet used to describe Molière as a libertine, and would play the part of the sweetshop-keeping uncle who sold sugar sticks and who dispensed moral teachings, in the children's plays of Berquin.[9]

It can thus be seen that this good-natured inhabitant of the province of Touraine was worthy of his renown; indeed, his qualities could even

5. Henri II of Navarre, also known as Henri d'Albret (1503-1555), waged an unsuccessful war against Ferdinand II of Aragon in an attempt to win back that part of the kingdom of Navarre which the latter had usurped. Henri belonged to a warlike family which held power over several centuries, eventually acceding to the French throne.

6. In the Hebrew Bible, the "coat of many colors" is the name for the possibly multicolored garment that Joseph owned; in the Old Testament's Book of Genesis, Joseph's father Jacob gave him the coat as a gift, to the envy of his brothers.

7. Urbain Grandier (1590–1634) was a French Catholic priest who was burned at the stake after being convicted of witchcraft, specifically, the events of the Loudun Possessions. In 1632, a group of nuns from the local Ursuline convent accused him of having bewitched them, sending the demon Asmodai, among others, to commit evil acts with them.

8. This is a further Biblical allusion to the story of Joseph in the Book of Genesis, who was allegedly seduced by the Pharaoh's wife in Egypt, but refused her advances, after which she accused him of rape and had him thrown into prison.

9. Arnaud Berquin (1747–1791) was an author, dramatist and teacher, the bulk of whose writings were directed at children. He is said to be the first French author to have specialized in children's literature. His books for children were very popular during his lifetime and were regularly reprinted throughout the 19th century. His works included plays for children with both moral and scientific instruction. As a popular writer who was enjoyed by younger readers as well as adults, and whose writings had, amongst other purposes, a pedagogical remit, perhaps Bequin could be regarded as a forerunner of, or literary influence on, Jules Verne.

be said to surpass his reputation. A man of simple tastes, discreet in all his undertakings and in all of his dealings with people, his virtues would have been sung by Horace[10] if he, Jamet, had lived in the era of Augustus[11]; however, fate had prevented the Tiber from echoing in refrain, with melodious voice, the name of the gentle Jédédias.

He was a man of slender proportions and of a rather chilling, offputting appearance! His face was sufficiently yellow for his family tree to be inscribed thereon; always freshly shaved, in Winter as in Summer, at daybreak he would invariably plunge, into a huge tub of cold water, the head supported by his puny shoulders. The small waistline was not exquisitely formed, and if, in his chaste imagination, he could have ever visualised such a thing as men's corsets; if his very proper torso had consented to donning this feminine attire, still he could not have acquired more harmonious proportions. There was no flexibility to be hoped for from his narrow hips, no springiness to be expected from the forbidding small of his back. Nature had fashioned him thus; one day, it had thrown some seeds in a field, and he had sprouted up like one of the palm trees of Mount Lebanon,[12] or one of the fir trees of the Northern countries, its leaves still all a-rustled by the melodious sounds of the Scottish bard.[13]

---

10. Horace, known in Latin as Quintus Horatius Flaccus (65 – 8 B.C.), was a Latin-language poet, born in the south of Italy.

11. Augustus (63 B.C. – 14 A.D.), known in Latin as Caius Octavius Thurinius, and also known as Octave and Octavian, was the first Roman emperor, and reigned during what is known as the Golden age of Roman literature, the era of such writers as Virgil, Horace and Ovide. This is the "golden age" referred to by Verne in this text.

12. Mount Lebanon is the Lebanese mountain range, also known as the Western Mountain Range of Lebanon. The mountains are known for their oak and pine forests. Also, in the high slopes of Mt Lebanon are the last remaining groves of the Cedars of Lebanon. Mt Lebanon is mentioned in the Old Testament several times; for instance, its Cedar wood was used to build the Jewish Temple of Jerusalem. This therefore seems to be another religious/Biblical reference (e.g. see footnotes 2 and 3).

13. This may be a reference to Ossian or Oisin, son of Fionn mac Cumhaill in Gaelic mythology, who supposedly wrote a long series of epic poems, translated into English in 1760 by the Scottish poet James Macpherson. However, the authenticity of the alleged originals has been questioned by scholars, so that Macpherson's work may be a form of pseudo-translation, drawn in reality from diverse sources.

In Roman times, he would have come in handy as a ballista[14] against the high walls of Carthage![15] Thus can one be made of ironwood, and yet be an honest man at the same time. [16]

Jédédias's arms belonged to those of the human race, and his legs clearly marked him out as the type of man defined by Plato[17] and parodied by Diogenes,[18] the Ham[19] of his time; but he would not have posed in any artist's studio. Forbidden to him were the specialities of a grumpy, cursing old man, of Christ on the cross, or of Holopherne[20] after his military operation; and short of posing as a mummy, he would hardly have enjoyed any modelling success at a rate of five francs per session, lighting not included.

Jamet can thus now be visualized quite plainly, in the cold light of

14. An ancient catapult used for hurling stones; an ancient form of large crossbow used to propel spears. In the original French text, the editor provides a footnote describing the ballista as "a war machine of Roman origin, which was used to fire arrows and other projectiles by means of a sloping, adjustable launching pad" (my translation).

15. Carthage refers to a series of cities on the Gulf of Tunis, from a Phoenician colony of the first millennium B.C. to the current suburb outside Tunis, Tunisia. In ancient times, the city had massive walls, 23 miles (37 kilometres) in length. Some of these walls were never penetrated by attackers.

16. The original French sentence is "On peut être de bois de fer, et honnête home tout à la fois." I have translated it literally; however, there may be an intended wordplay, one which is perhaps almost impossible to translate, in Verne's original, in that the juxtaposition of "bois de fer" and "honnête" to describe Jamet may be a humorous, polysemous allusion to the French saying or "comptine" ("children's rhyme") "Croix de bois, croix de fer, si je mens je vais en enfer," which is equivalent to the English phrase "Cross my heart and hope to die."

17. Plato (428/427 – 347/346 B.C.) was a Greek philosopher and disciple of Socrates.

18. Diogenes, a Greek poet and doxographer (one who collects the opinions and conjectures of ancient Greek philosophers), is thought to have lived in the 3rd century A.D.

19. Ham (Cham in the original French) was the second son of Noah, in the Book of Genesis, and is said to have been born when Noah was already 500 years old, prior to the Flood. He was the brother of Shem and Japhet, and is said to be the ancestor of the dark-skinned African races.

20. This is a further Biblical reference. Holopherne, whose story is recounted in the Book of Judith, was an Old Testament general who was sent on a military campaign by Nebuchadnezzar and later decapitated by Judith.

day, without any dressing, as it were; and as he is a comic sort of fellow, one should not be fearful of approaching people fitting this description, with such words as: "Oh hello there, Jédédias, how's the form?"

Indeed, the police do not forbid you from giving them a tap on the belly.

This apparently faultless gentleman did, however, possess one defect, albeit a defect of excessive scrupulosity. This fault was hardly more than a virtue taken to an extreme, a type of inordinate neatness; M. Jamet was so fastidious in his tidiness, that he could not conceive of the wear and tear of any garment!

Each morning, he would spend several hours brushing, shining and pressing a dark coat, a professional outfit which had been handed down to him from his father, who had been a bailiff[21] of modest means in the little town of Chambéry. This was all he had been able to recuperate from the paternal inheritance, his minimum legal entitlement; in short, his rightful but mediocre legacy.[22]

At first glance, a coat worn by a rather rotund, greasy bailiff, must seem to resemble its master; rubbed against the wooden benches of the 'legal-eagle' bailiffs and clerks of the court,[23] worn threadbare in the

---

21. The French term used by Verne in the original text, to describe the profession of Jamet's late father, is "huissier à verge," which literally translates as "a bailiff with a rod, or wand of office," the "verge" thus being an emblem of authority, a sort of badge of office. The original text has an editor's footnote stating that the term formerly referred to royal sergeants received at Chatelet. Chatelet was a Parisian seat of justice and a prison.

22. Just as this text is peppered with historical, mythological and religious allusions, so too does it contain several legal terms; Verne was, at the time he wrote this text, studying law in Paris, as his father, a lawyer in Nantes, wanted him to eventually take over the family law practice. The French terms employed by Verne here to describe Jamet's meagre vestmental inheritance are "sa réserve, sa légitimité." The "réserve héreditaire/légale," a legal term dating from 1636, is defined by the *Petit Robert* (2007: 2212) as (and I translate) the "portion of an inheritance which is reserved by law to certain heirs." The term "légitimité" has a similar meaning: in older French law, dating back to 1562, "la légitime" was an institution charged with protecting "legitimate heirs" by ensuring they obtained a portion of an inheritance. (ibid: 1441). Jamet would thus have been described in French as an "héritier réservataire" or "héritier légitime."

23. The original text provides an editorial footnote explaining that the term used here by Verne, "basoche," was formerly used to designate the entire assemblage of clerks of the courts of justice, united in professional organizations, and that it has pejorative connotations when used to refer to lawyers, solicitors, bailiffs and

midst of the fragrant masses who arrive to moralize to each other at the criminal courts, torn to shreds during seizures of too much moveable property[24], it would thus seem to be fit only for the sack of the rag-and-bone man, that great street philosopher, or suitable only to adorn the back of a solicitor's clerk; but the honest bailiff, guided by his integrity rather than personal advantage, had only ever been involved in rather inconsequential legal cases in the native province of Vaugelas[25] and of the abbot of Saint-Réal[26]. Upon his death, fruitless searches had been made for any records of private income which he might have had from Government stocks, five per cent consolidated or otherwise; for shares in the railways of northern France, or securities in banks in London, Amsterdam or Berlin. His creditors, to whom were owed both secured and unsecured loans,[27] the endorsees, the legal beneficiaries, all rapidly descended, like the fifth plague of Egypt,[28] on the will as it went through probate[29]. The bakers, undertakers' assistants, butchers, parish church

---

other members of the legal profession. As Verne's satirical text probably intended to convey this derogatory sense of the term, I have inserted the qualifier "legal-eagle" in an attempt to secure some kind of equivalent depreciatory effect.

24. The original French legal term used by Verne, "saisies…mobilières," refers to the seizure of goods by distraint, for sale, in the execution of a court order.

25. Claude Favre de Vaugelas, baron of Pérouges and lord of Vaugelas (1585-1650) was a grammarian, and one of the first members of the Académie Française.

26. César Vichard de Saint-Réal (1639-1692) was a French writer who covered several genres, but who is perhaps best known for his historical writings.

27. The legal terms in the original text are "les créanciers hypothécaires, les créanciers chirographaires." The former term refers to loans which are secured by a Deed of Mortgage as executed by a solicitor; the latter, to loans which "lack the security – often, the notarial deed – giving a right of preference to a creditor in enforcing the debtor's commitments" (*Petit Robert*, 2007: 422, my translation). The original text offers a footnote explaining that the legal term "chirographies" applies to a person who is unable to prove what is legally due to him, except by means of an Affidavit, as there is no Deed or Indenture witnessed by a solicitor.

28. The Ten Plagues of Egypt, also known as the Biblical Plagues, are the ten calamities visited upon Egypt by Yahweh (Exodus, Chapters 7-12) to convince Pharaoh to free the Israelite slaves. The fifth plague, the Plague of Livestock Death (Ex. 9:1-7) was an epidemic disease which exterminated Egyptian livestock, i.e. horses, donkeys, camels, cattle, sheep and goats, while the Israelite's cattle were left unharmed.

29. The term used in Verne's original is "succession de cujus," also referred to as a "succession ouverte," meaning a deceased person's estate as it is being probated.

DEWITT COMMUNITY LIBRARY

trustees, the tailor and the solicitor, all flung themselves like a plague of locusts upon the poor furnishings which affected to adorn the bereaved household, and the poor heir, in a pitiful, sorry state,[30] legally obliged to constitute the continuing legal person of the deceased, could not suppose that there was anything better to claim, other than to attire himself in the aforementioned grease-stained, cast-off vestment.

The Land Registry took only a proportionate amount of inheritance tax on the value of the estate.

Now that he was, finally, the owner of the paternal coat, Jédédias Jamet, being a dutiful and meticulous son, had his inheritance lined and turned inside out by the best tailor in the town. This tailor, as roguish as an old-fashioned workman, wore a subtle smile as he returned the transformed garment, the masterpiece of his imagination and of his scissors, to its owner and occupier, Jamet.

"Monsieur Jédédias," said he to Jamet, "this coat will last longer than yourself, provided it doesn't get ripped to shreds before you die!"

The native of Touraine, momentarily alarmed at seeing his life expectancy jeopardized to such an extent, gave a witty rejoinder to the shiftily sniggering, malicious clothier: "Well, it'll be ripped to pieces, that's what I think!"

This tailor was German, a native of the town of Gartz in Pomerania, and, on the banks of the Oder, he had drawn those fresh sources of inspiration which were his distinctive quality.

Jédédias Jamet donned, forthwith, the inheritance from his father the bailiff; and when, several years later, having become wealthy as a result of an inheritance from one of his cousins, an intrepid aviator who had dropped himself from a height of three thousand metres, Jédédias offered his heart and coat-sleeve to Miss Perpetua Tertullien. He was approved by her family, who were duly touched by the proposal. Every evening since then, he had carefully folded in four the coat to which he owed his happiness, while each morning he would retrieve it once more, in order to go about his day-to-day business.

But what sort of care and attention did he lavish upon this coat? It would be more appropriate to ask what did he *not* do to take care of it.

---

30. Verne here uses the term "marmiteux." A footnote in the French original says that this is an old-fashioned and colloquial term meaning that somebody is "pathetic; a person to whom fate has not been kind" (my translation).

He would not tolerate so much as an inquisitive fly coming along with its miniscule feelers to rummage about in the depths of this prehistoric woollen garment.[31] In any case, the unfortunate insect in question, as young Francis used to point out in a most scholarly manner, would have found, in that coat, not the tiniest morsel of birdseed or the smallest worm.[32]

We are led to believe that such a fly would, however, have met, on Jamet Junior's jacket, a neighbour to whom she could tell her tales of woe!

Monsieur Jédédias, who wore nothing out, did, however, wear out his brushes.

When he had carefully attired himself in his coat, in accordance with the rules of applied geometry of the thumb and index finger, he would gracefully roll up the facing side of the sleeves, thus making visible his shirt which was happy to see the light of day; then, with a gentle and skilfully aimed flick of his fingers, he would cause to fly faraway from the cuffs, coat-tails and collar, those microcosmic specks which he alone could discern.

His attentiveness gradually extended to the more commonplace waistcoat and trousers; the former, tailored with double stitching and buttoned squarely, joined up with and matched the white tie which wound around Jédédias' neck. Monsieur Jamet looked like a barrister who was just about to take an oath, and each time he raised his hand

---

31. Verne here describes the woollen garment as "cet Elbeuf antédiluvien" ("that antediluvian Elbeuf"): Elbeuf, a town with a population of approximately 17,000 people (2005), situated in the Seine-Maritime department, in north-western France, is one of the traditional French centres of wool and cloth manufacture.

32. In the original, Verne writes "le plus petit grain de mil ou de vermisseau," which I have translated exactly; this reference by young Francis Jamet is said, ironically, by the narrator, to be scholarly, probably because it seems to be an attempted (but inaccurate) quotation from a poem by Jean de la Fontaine, *La Cigale et la Fourmi*, often translated as *The Grasshopper and the Ant*, which contains the lines "Pas un seul petit morceau/De mouche ou de vermisseau" (literally, "Not a single little morsel/ Of fly or tiny worm"). Jean de la Fontaine (1621–1695) was the most famous French fabulist (a person who invents or recounts fables) and one of the most widely read poets of the 17th century, still much read today. There are many very free translations of this particular fable into English (adapted for the sake of achieving rhyme in English) but one of the more literal and thus highly close, accurate renderings, entitled *The Cicada and the Ant*, can be found on the website http://www.jdlf.com/lesfables/livrei/lacigaleetlafourmi/?pp=1.

toward the heavens, with his measured gestures, one almost felt one could hear the formal words *I do swear* issuing forth from his mouth.

The pantaloons, which were of a shiny and polished black, plainly revealed, by means of a fly which was properly buckled with three metal buttons, their mythical origins, which dated back to the last days of the Golden Age of the Roman empire. One's mind was automatically cast back to the siege of Troy, to the misfortunes of Actaeon[33] and the laws of Lycurgus[34]; this essential attire, the very name of which is a shocking affront to the modest sensibilities of English ladies, fluttered unchecked several centimetres above Monsieur Jamet's ankles, while a shoe, mathematically laced with a dark cotton thread, heavily trod the yielding ground, completing Jédédias' lower extremities in a completely web-footed manner.

The reader is asked to excuse these minute details of dress; one cannot, of course, judge the book by its cover, and it is an irrefutable truth that clerical dress does not the monk maketh. Rather, the monk maketh the robe; but as Nature had not bestowed any other vice on Jédédias, and as his excessive tidiness could only be regarded as an odd but completely inoffensive obsession, it has been necessary to depict this individual through his eccentricities.

Chapter II

In which it shall be seen that M. Jédédias Jamet was not quick to anger, and that he used to give lessons in calligraphy to young Francis, while the beautiful Joséphine would exercise her little fingers on the keyboard.

Monsieur Jamet was a fine man, and not merely a harmless little old fellow.[35] He had his own personality, just like any other individual,

---

33. In Greek mythology, Actaeon, having suffered the fatal wrath of Artemis, was transformed into a stag and torn apart by raging hounds.

34. Lycurgus of Sparta (800? – 730 B.C.?) was the legendary lawgiver who established the military-oriented reformation of Spartan society in accordance with the Oracle of Apollo at Delphi. All of his reforms were aimed at achieving the three Spartan virtues of equality among citizens, military fitness and austerity.

35. There is wordplay in the original which is difficult to reproduce in English, viz. "Monsieur Jamet était un homme bon, et non pas un bonhomme."

and was given to reflection, to a greater extent than might have been supposed from his appearance. Fair, but rigid and unyielding, he always walked straight ahead toward his goal without varying his trajectory by so much as a line; the entreaties of a frantic spouse or tearful mother would not have exerted any influence over his decisions. Not as strong as Brutus, he would nonetheless have slain his son as a sacrificial offering, if he had possessed another one; incapable of squashing a fly unnecessarily, or of piercing a butterfly for no legitimate purpose, he would have willingly given the blood of his nearest and dearest in order to spare a drop of his own.[36] These sentiments, cruel though they may initially seem, did not have their source in the unreachable mountains of Egoism; they were, rather, the natural consequence of an essentially methodical mind, one which would not give you the parsley off its fish or willingly incur any unnecessary expense.

When faced with difficult situations, he had always displayed an imperturbability worthy of the heroic age, and the local newspapers had, on numerous occasions, reason to report on his incredible presence of mind.

One day, he was walking along his usual roadway, inwardly deliberating as to whether he could apply the properties of the hypotenuse to the darning of cotton hems; he was already close to finding the solution to this important problem, when piercing screams suddenly became audible from behind a copse of trees. He directed his steps with a measured pace toward the source of the cries, in his customarily unhurried fashion; indeed, Madame Perpetua née Romuald Tertullien would vouch for the fact that he was never rushed under any circumstances. He arrived at the bank of the river whose current, skilfully retained by barriers, powered a mill situated lower down the riverbank. An elderly, though respectable lady there heaved harrowing sighs; these were undoubtedly the tears of a mother who found herself in desperate straits. This respectable, though elderly, woman was exhorting a young shepherd to jump into the deep water, through promises of financial reward!

"There'll be no more time left! Hector," she cried, "Hector, I've lost you! If only I was a man, Hector! Hector! If only I was Achilles!" [37]

---

36. Lucius Junius Brutus was the legendary founder of the Roman Republic. He was said to have condemned his own sons to death and to have attended their execution.

37. In Greek mythology, Achilles was a Greek hero of the Trojan War, the central character and the greatest warrior of Homer's *Illiad*. Later legends state that

Monsieur Jédédias Jamet, whose ruminations had been disrupted by this completely anti-mythological juxtaposition of proper names, approached, with an air of desperation, the woman who was writhing in distress.

"What sorrow is thine?," he exclaimed, striking a classic pose.

"Ah! You are my savior! You are Achilles, sir! Make this good-for-nothing tearaway ashamed," she went on, pointing to the indecisive shepherd who was swaying awkwardly from side to side, leaning on his crook.

"You are in mourning for somebody," went on Monsieur Jamet!

"Help! Help! Don't you see Hector being carried off by the strong current?"

"To the left, down there?"

"No, to the right."

"Can he swim?"

"Very poorly, sir, very poorly!"

"It's likely that he shall drown!"

"It's a certainty! It's a certainty! Allow me, sir, to undress you…"

"Madam!" cried Jédédias, in the tone of voice used by Napoleon to Princess Josephine, prior to his divorce.[38]

The poor mother had already placed a maternal but defiling hand on the spotless collar of the famous coat!

Monsieur Jamet gently pushed her away, flicked particles from the different parts of his garment, directed a satisfied look at it, and resuming his cleaning:

"Madam!" he said, throwing far away from his dark shoe, a protozoan which had chosen to take up residence there.

"My dog! My poor Hector!" howled the despairing mother.

"It's only a dog?"

"*Only* a dog?" repeated the mother, in a fury.

"Is there a one hundred *sou* coin to make it worth my while to rescue him, all the same?" continued the young shepherd, who had by now considered the matter.

"Two coins, young fellow, two!"

Achilles was invulnerable in all of his body except for his heel, and that he died due to an arrow shot into his heel.

38. Napoleon I (Napoleon Bonaparte) (1769–1821) was a military and political leader of France. His first wife was Joséphine de Beauharnais.

"Done!"

And the shepherd began to undress, paying no attention to the women who surrounded him, as a number of people had, by this time, begun to gather on the river bank.

But a mother in tears, and the women who observe her, have no time to gaze at shameless objects!

The poor dog was struggling as best he could in the cold water, and was coming considerably closer to the lock, situated upriver from the mill.

The young shepherd, now naked and bursting with energy, was about to plunge himself into the river, when Jédédias Jamet held him back, with a discreet touch of his hand.

"You reckless young madman, you're rushing to your death!"

"Nay!"

"Shepherd!"

"Sir, what do you think you're getting yourself involved in?" continued the mother, now worked up into an overexcited state. "Hector! Hector!"

"Madame!"

"I'm holding you responsible for all this!"

"Do I dive in or what?" the naked shepherd stuttered.

"There is no need whatsoever!"

"Sir! Help! Hector!"

"Madame, listen to me!"

"Hector! Can you hear me?"

"I'm being cool, calm and collected…"

"And I'm not exactly overheated," murmured the nude shepherd.

"There is absolutely no need…"

"Keep quiet, you wretch."

"To dive into the water!"

"Hector!"

"We shall get him back…"

"What right do you have to kill Hector?"

"Once he gets near to the lock!"

"Do you really think so?," the somewhat mellowed mother went on, a ray of hope having crept right into her heart.

"I am certain of it," Jédédias Jamet triumphantly replied, and he slowly directed his steps toward the mill, while the feet of the onlookers had by now been given wings, thanks to their tenderness and curiosity.

The dog, whose strength was beginning to wane, began to offer battle with the current formed by the narrowing of the barriers, and soon disappeared under the mill wheel, which had not stopped turning.

When Monsieur Jédédias Jamet arrived close to the lock, the crushed and lifeless body of Hector was in repose on the grass, while echoes reverberated, in long moans, of the grief of the poor mother, who, on seeing Jédédias, cried: "This is all your doing!," whereupon she fell unconscious to the ground.

"Ladies and gentlemen," Monsieur Jamet responded, his voice trembling with emotion, and turning round to face the onlookers, "We could have recovered him alive, we have retrieved him dead, but, just as I had predicted, we have certainly got him back!"

Needless to say, the elderly and respectable lady was not Hector's real mother, but this sweet appellation had been bestowed upon her because of the children she did have or could have!

The story of these events caused a sensation throughout the Sologne region, and the newspapers of Romorantin recounted them, portraying Monsieur Jédédias Jamet in a most favorable light, and proposing him as a candidate at the forthcoming elections.

As might be supposed, Monsieur Jamet, thanks to his newfound renown, which had been acquired by word of·mouth, quickly became the oracle of the locality! On a daily basis, people from within a radius of several decameters would come to consult him, and, indeed, this rightfully acquired fame of Monsieur Jamet was causing Monsieur Honoré Rabutin, royal attorney, to lose his halo.[39]

Already, and through following the excellent advice of Monsieur Jamet, firefighters who had hastened to a scene in the nick of time, had allowed several farms to burn; numerous harvests had failed because the locals were relying on monsieur Jamet's almanac; many people had been killed while out hunting, because the hunters fired in a diagonal direction which had been taught to them by that exemplary gentleman, while whole herds had perished from smallpox, from which

---

39. On checking whether the Rabutin referred to here by Verne was an actual person, the only Rabutin to whom I could find reference was Roger de Rabutin, Comte de Bussy (1618–1693), a French writer of memoirs.

they had not been suffering, because they had gorged themselves on medicines introduced to the region by the nephew of Opime Romuald Tertullien.

The local farmers were happy and would graciously salute their idol when, descending from his pedestal, he would take a walk through the lands surrounding his country residence, which was situated three leagues from Amboise, on the fortunate banks of the Loire.

These pastoral preoccupations could not, however, divert Monsieur Jédédias from his habits of propriety; thus was he never to be seen compromising his reputation among the drunken and dung-stained throngs of village revellers; he would never condescend to mingle with the crowds at open-air dances, made golden by the last vestiges of evening sunlight! No, he would have feared for the virginal lustre of his vestments, and just as a dread-afflicted mother keeps her daughter captive under her wing, so too did he live in dread of any base or obscene fondling of the sole object of his thoughts.

Moreover, should there ever occur, by happenstance, one of those unavoidable accidents which testify to the excellence of the social condition, he would first of all repair the damage with a composure which Mucius Scaevola would have envied, and only afterwards would he become angry.[40]

Should a carriage of the nobility or of the bourgeoisie, be it lavish or wretched, with tong-shaped springs or otherwise, happen to splash him, he would slip into a murky alley under cover of darkness, and there, through the anxious and restorative appliance of a handkerchief, he would reinvest the defiled part of his garment with its original splendor, and only then would he indulge in self-recrimination for having ventured outside in such weather!

"It's pouring like a razor!"

This was the extremely pretty and one and only witty turn of phrase that he allowed himself, despite not understanding it! Having berated himself, he would then begin to rebuke the heavens for the accident of which he had been a victim, and finally, he would sharply

---

40. Gaius Mucius Scaevola was a noble and probably mythical Roman youth, renowned for his bravery. When the Etruscan king Lars Porsenna ordered him to be cast into flames, Mucius stoically accepted this punishment, pre-empting Porsenna by thrusting his hand into the fire and showing no signs of pain. Porsenna, impressed by the young man's bravery, freed him.

refer to the unfortunate coachman against whom his complaint was directed, as a clumsy, improper oaf!

If a clock fell on his head, he considered himself fortunate to have greeted, at the moment of the free fall, a person of his acquaintance, and to have thus avoided, at the expense of his cranial canvas, the flattening intended for his hat.

In a word, the collisions of carts, the pushing and scuffling of tardy porters, the lashes of the whips of the mail-coach postillions, found him obediently faithful to his rules of conduct, and when, the damage having been repaired, he would burst forth into a torrent of infuriated invectives, the cart had already been brought back to its destination, the porter had gotten back to the wine merchant and the postillion was three post-stops away from the scene of the incident.

Moreover, his more or less emphatic use of "Clumsy oaf!" was sufficient for his personal and daily consumption of insults, and the most traditional purists of the Académie Française could never have found reason to reprimand him for his means of expressing astonishment during these critical moments of existence.

On only one occasion did a horrid street urchin cause him to depart from the limits of the dictionary. This teenage boy had driven a stake into the ground and had delicately placed, on its upper part, a small plank which was not any more than a foot in length; this horizontally positioned piece of wood thus tipping back and forth, the young stream-dweller had placed, at one end of it, a foul, disgusting toad which had been picked up several months previously in the muddy terrain of a neighboring sandpit! Having breathed its last several days before, the poor creature was no longer capable of evoking any pity from the idle and unsympathetic passers-by. Once this contraption had been built, the beastly young whippersnapper, with a heavy stick at the end of his strong arm, struck that part of the plank which was bereft of all things reptilian, thereby sending the toad's wretched remains flying upwards, toward the vault of the heavens.

The weather was glorious, and the spring sunshine, radiating its gentle heat, had enticed the bourgeoisie to inhale the fresh air of the great outdoors. Monsieur Jédédias Jamet was taking his customary stroll, his umbrella under his arm, with the air of a contented man, when his hat suddenly seemed to give way under the pressure of a foreign body, of which he did not, at first, realise the nature; feeling alarmed, he placed his hand on the injured extremity and recognized, with easily understandable revulsion, the type of 'rainfall' he was dealing with! The whole universe seemed to flash before his eyes; but before rejoicing in this rare phenomenon, he let out a terrible cry:

"Pig! You dirty pig!"

He then returned home, his head not as lost as his hat. He treated, as best he could, the odorous wound which the heavens, or so he imagined, had visited upon him, and went to bed without dinner in order to stew, in comfort, in his justifiable indignation.

This had been the darkest episode of his existence, one which he could not, and should not, forget!

Should the reader find it astonishing that special mention has not heretofore been made of Jédédias Jamet's hat, this is because it is due to form the subject matter of a separate chapter of its own.

Since the occurrence of this incident, monsieur Jamet had resumed his customary existence; he taught young Francis to write, cutting his quills with rare perfection.

He did continue to fly into the occasional fit of agitation, now and then, as a result of ink stains fired by the careless quill of his budding son and heir; but there are no limits to the suffering which a father is prepared to endure in the name of the moral and religious instruction of his children.

Young Francis was not exactly hungry for knowledge of the straight and sloping downstrokes of his handwriting lessons, but it was necessary that he be educated, and his father, never given to joking, certainly did not view his son's education as any laughing matter. As soon as he had cut and shaped the household quills, he would put away his pocket knife in a double-locked desk, and would catch hold of the scholastic and paternal birch-rod; and thus did master Francis, whether he liked it or not, set out on the roadway to scientific knowledge, trodden of yore by such as Newton and Lavoisier.[41]

As for madame Perpetua Jamet, who in the halcyon days of her childhood had won a certificate of merit for coming in fifth place at a piano examination, she gave motherly keyboard lessons, free of charge,

---

41. Sir Issac Newton F.R.S. (1643–1727) was an English physicist, mathematician, astronomer, natural philosopher, alchemist and theologian, and is considered by many scholars to be one of the most influential people in human history. Antoine Lavoisier (1743–1794) known as the "father of modern chemistry," was a French nobleman prominent in the disciplines of chemistry and biology.

to the beautiful Joséphine. This young lady was the spitting image of her mother, but completely different in appearance from Monsieur Jédédias; however, the virtue of Romuald Tertullien's niece was so well established, that not a single spoofer had ever dared to draw the logical inferences of this physical dissimilarity.

And so, the days of this simple and honest family were taken up with clothing, handwriting and harpsichord.

But what singular, unforeseen contingency was to cause monsieur Jédédias Jamet to be abruptly dragged from obscurity and plunged into the midst of events and setbacks far removed from his usual sphere of activity?

Chapter III

In which it is explained how Madame Perpetua Jamet was a member of the Romuald Tertullien family, and how Monsieur Romuald Tertullien was her uncle.

"Madame Jamet! Madame Jamet! Is Madame Jamet ever going to come here? Such an event! An event of this nature! An event of this kind! Madame Jamet! This sudden, unexpected death! But this must be a fortune which is falling upon us from the skies, and the only things that usually ever fall from there are rain and aeroliths![42] Madame Jamet, Perpetua! Will you please come here at once, I tell you!"

Thus did Monsieur Jédédias shout, thrashing about like a cat on a hot tin roof, as he continued to read and reread the famous letter announcing the death of his uncle Opime Romuald Tertullien.

"What on earth is your mother doing?" asked Monsieur Jamet of young Francis.

"I don't know," replied the small boy, who was otherwise occupied, in the toilet adjoining the marital bedroom!

"He must have been extremely wealthy, this top-ranking merchant! But who in the name of God could have written this letter to me? Madame Jamet! Madame Jamet!"

---

42. Aeroliths are stony meteorites consisting of silicate minerals. Perhaps this scientific/ geological reference is an early indication of what would become one of Verne's central literary themes, scientific pedagogy and references to natural science.

And Monsieur Jédédias's voice seemed to possess uncustomary tones!

"Francis, go and fetch your mother!"

And Monsieur Jédédias, with a strangely grasping, greedy expression in his eyes, studied the black-bordered epistle as though it were some kind of mysterious parchment.

"This absence of relatives to whom to announce the death of Opime Tertullien proves that we are the only successors; we're the only ones who could have forwarded this announcement to our friends and acquaintances! I say, Francis, have you gone to fetch your mother?"

"I can't!" replied a muffled voice that seemed to be carried from a distance, like that of a ventriloquist!

"You can't, you little brat? How did I come to have such a tearaway for a son? Francis!"

"Um…"

"Francis! What are you playing at in that bathroom?"

"Yesterday, I ate too many strawberries with cream and it's given me a pain in my stomach!"

"You accursed child! Are you going to obey me?"

"But I can't!"

"Francis!"

And young Francis emerged in an appalling state; luckily, his long childhood smock concealed, with due propriety, the offensive disarray of a certain activity, rudely interrupted!

"But where the hell did this Opime live?" wondered Monsieur Jamet.

At this moment, Madame Perpetua arrived, rebuking young Francis for coming to fetch her while he was in such a state.

"That damned brat, will you look at the state of him!"

"But it was Papa who…"

"Be quiet!"

"Madame Jamet, come here, will you, come here! Will you read this, I say!"

With these words, Monsieur Jamet placed under her eyes, the cause of his unaccustomed overexcitement.

As for young Francis, caught in the crossfire but pursued by an even more compelling adversary, he had immediately withdrawn into the bathroom, ensuring to judiciously close the door.

"Well, what do you say to this? What do you think, wife?"

"It's unbelievable!"

"But this piece of news can hardly have been fabricated!"

"Poor Uncle Opime Tertullien," said Madame Perpetua, going to fetch a white handkerchief.

"Poor? Hardly, I should think! On the contrary, he must have been filthy rich! These big businessmen live on nothing, they eat the packaging of their merchandise, and become heavy and fat! What an unexpected stroke of good fortune this is, Madame Perpetua!"

"You seem to be taking the news of this death very cheerfully," said the tender-hearted niece of the deceased gentleman, doing her utmost to shed tears, so as not to have to avow a cruel hardness of heart to her confessor.

"But no, no, of course," resumed Monsieur Jédédias, "But no, that good uncle…Truly this is a misfortune for the family…But after all…! When one has children to provide for…A fortune is something worthy of esteem! Ah! Heavens above! This is too bad; but I don't feel like moaning: I'll cry tomorrow!"

The excellent gentleman was unable to conceal his joy, which escaped from his being as water might issue from a watering can.

"Where did this uncle reside?"

"We've heard nothing about him for the last ten years!"

"But where was it he lived?"

"He lived in Rotterdam!"

"Rotterdam! In Holland?"

"I suppose so!"

"Well, we'll soon know what we're dealing with here!"

"Who sent us this letter?"

"What does it matter? Perhaps it was sent upon the instructions of the deceased. That seems quite plausible! But the important thing is that uncle Opine is dead!"

In the course of that morning, the honest Jédédias had committed more murders than is appropriate for a decent man.

Oh! Jamet, if only you had known then, the tribulations you were to endure, as the penalty payable for your reprehensible trust!

"My hat," said Monsieur Jamet.

Madame Perpetua recoiled in horror! It was the first time that Jédédias had made a request of this nature! Given that he had never before, in living memory, allowed the desecrating hand of another to soil his ancient felt hat, he must no longer be in full possession of his faculties!

"Where are you going?" enquired Madame Perpetua, who was all a-trembling.

"To my solicitor, monsieur Honoré Rabutin. I shall give him a thorough explanation of our genealogy and seek his advice! Goodbye; don't expect me for lunch! Or, perhaps, for dinner either! Don't even expect me tomorrow! Kiss me, Perpetua, and pray for me; for I know not when I shall return! Adieu! Adieu!"

And he exited like a madman, knocking over, in the drawing room, the piano stool on which the beautiful Joséphine was suffering boredom, rehearsing as she had been for the last two years, the same study by Czerny; he then knocked down the cook who was sweeping the antechamber, and practically fell into the street, like Achilles, obtaining victory amongst Agamemnon's soldiers, at the tip of his double-edged sword![43]

Monsieur Jédédias Jamet quickly breezed through the residential district, with a rapidity of foot just about equal to that of Aeneas fleeing a burning Troy; all of the local residents had stationed themselves at their windows, and remained stupefied because he had opened his umbrella, in spite of the fact that, at that very moment, the only things raining down were joyous rays of sunshine.[44] News of this bizarre behavior quickly spread throughout the whole town; nobody seemed to know to what cause this emotional display of Jamet could be attributed; groups of people began to form at the crossroads; the Guard (with very little of the 'National' about it) took up arms in its fright, and that evening, the following report appeared in the newspapers:

"It is thought that the navigation of the Loire is about to be interrupted; there is reason to believe that the barge-arch of the bridge of Cé has collapsed, between the hours of eight and nine o'clock

---

43. In Greek mythology, Agamemnon was the son of King Atreus of Mycenae and Queen Aerope. He was the commander-in-chief of the Greeks during the Trojan War. He took an attractive slave from Achilles. The latter, the greatest warrior of his age, withdrew from battle in revenge and almost cost the Greek armies the war.

44. At the fall of Troy, Aeneas, who had been Leader of the Dardanians during the Trojan War, left the city in flames, and after wandering in the Mediterranean Sea, came to Italy and founded the state that later became Rome.

this morning. This bridge, as we know, had been constructed by the Romans, a fact which accounts for its lack of stability; the uncustomary upheaval of Monsieur Jédédias Jamet, who failed to win a seat at the last elections, has given rise to this event!"

Within a matter of moments, the new heir had arrived at the home of his solicitor, Honoré Rabutin, and rang at the door with such violence that the doorbell broke, without having had the time to render any sound! The visitor's cries soon led to the door being opened.

Despite the fact that he was a solicitor, Monsieur Honoré Rabutin was, at that moment, taking a morning bath; he was playing like a child in his bathtub, amusing himself through his attempts to submerge, within the yellowish water, a certain amount of air which was compressed within a fold of his bathrobe. He described this activity as 'making little cowpats'.

Suddenly, an ill-timed, inopportune intruder rushed headlong into his beloved refuge; he scarcely had time to cover his breast by placing, across it, the wet garment worn by bathers, and to conceal from the feverish eyes of his client, his registered and notarized perfections. If he had been Diana, Monsieur Jédédias Jamet, like the grandson of Cadmus, would have been devoured by his own dogs; though it is true that he had only a skinny, constipated cat, whose ablutions Madame Perpetua performed each morning with soap and water.[45]

"Excuse me, Monsieur Rabutin, but here's what has just happened to me," thundered Jédédias, foaming at the mouth. "What's your opinion of this case? Have you sometimes seen inheritances bequeathed on clients out of the blue, in such an unexpected manner? Do you think there could be other beneficiaries besides myself? When I say 'myself', I actually mean my wife, as she is a Romuald Tertullien; must I relinquish this inheritance? Must I accept it completely, or simply without liability to debts? If there are other beneficiaries, have they not had time to penalize my inheritance by imposing a statutory limitation on the time in which I can claim it? Do you think Monsieur Opime Tertullien has made a will? And how do you explain the care he has taken to notify me of his death? Was the letter written while he was still alive, and can it

---

45. Diana was the goddess of the hunt, and is associated with wild animals and woodland, and was also goddess of the moon in Roman mythology. As noted in an earlier footnote, Diana transformed Acteon into a stag and set his own hunting dogs to kill him.

not be considered as proof of the deceased's intentions? Could he have exercised a similar degree of care to send much the same type of epistle to unknown relatives? How closely related does one have to be, to the testator, in order to be legally entitled to inherit? Must I leave immediately, or do I have to wait for a second notification? No I don't, isn't that so? Because there are two possibilities: either Monsieur Romuald is alive or he's dead; if he is still living, he will not repeat a hoax of this nature; or else he is dead, in which case he will not be writing to me again; therefore, in either scenario, I could be waiting underneath the elm tree and I'd be waiting a long time! But, you may say to me, it is possible that he may still be alive. Who is to say that he hasn't died since sending this letter, which I would then regard as a malevolent communication, if it weren't for the respect owing to uncles from whom one inherits! That, as of today, he is legally, morally and ecclesiastically deceased, and that I must hurry to collect his bequest! Could the State not seek to lay claim to it, and take it from me as an unclaimed estate, an estate in abeyance? What statutory provision regulates this type of Government robbery? Have you ever had heard tell of a Church of Saint Colette the hip-swayer? Why was this hip-swayer called Colette, or, better phrased, why did this Colette wiggle her hips, and, above all, a question which is of paramount importance as it may put us on the right track, where did this Saint Colette ever wiggle her hips? And if this Opime person is still alive, can he not be sentenced to death, for damages occasioned by the upset which has been produced by this fraudulent letter? But speak, will you, answer me! You Anadyomenian solicitor!"[46]

Thus did the honest Jédédias orate; the heavens had just bestowed upon him a quality which he had not previously possessed, but one which he now shared with many pieces of hydraulic or gas-operated equipment: he was in full flow.

Though his bath had, by this time, become completely cold, the shivering and blue-complexioned Honoré Rabutin still had not leave to exit from his icebox; he was obliged to hear a complete account of the ancestry of Madame Jamet, and her thousand and one reasons for being a close relative and successor of Uncle Opime Romuald Tertullien.

---

46. In Verne's original French, Jamet addresses the solicitor as "Notaire anadyomène!" Venus Anadyomene means "Venus Rising From the Sea" and was one of the iconic representations of Aphrodite: the image represents the birth of Aphrodite, Goddess of Love, as she emerges from the waters.

And that is what he learned from the permanently opened mouth of the tireless Jédédias, who, far from sending a senior magistrate to sleep, would instead have woken him up.

[Verne's Outline of the conclusion of *Jédédias Jamet*]

Jamet had never had any news of his wife's uncle. He had never even seen this uncle—when her brother Vilfrid died, he claimed his inheritance, without, most certainly, hearing tell of her uncle Opime… therefore, he will go to Rotterdam to try to track him down; once there, however, he will meet nobody, apart from a solicitor who will inform him that it is true that M. Opime did live in Rotterdam, but that for the last four years he has been missing, having disappeared into thin air, and that nothing has ever been heard of him since. The solicitor will also tell him that he does not know where this Church of St Colette the Hip-Swayer is located, and that M. Opime had announced, just prior to his departure, that he had to go to A. Monsieur Jamet will then take into his service a timorous and food-loving boy, whose loyalty and skill have been highly recommended to him, and will set off from Rotterdam to A. in the mountains, where there will be an incident involving robbers—but there, still no sign of either Opime or of St Colette…he will be sent to B., where M. Opime had bought a property…he will go to B., and will take the property owner to be his uncle, and will wish to become acquainted with this 'uncle's' sentiments before becoming a [shipowner], [] story. He will then be sent to C., where his uncle was the hero of a tragic adventure; at C., he will meet some of Opime Tertullien's heirs, who will have nothing more urgent to do than to have him pursued as the nephew of their uncle. He will flee, in shirt sleeves, to D., where the faithful servant will bring him back his collection of plant illustrations; at D., still no trace of Opime, apart from a letter from him, which apparently says that, if, in four years, he has not made any communication, a letter which he had entrusted to his representative was to be opened—the letter is duly opened, and in it, Opime announces that he is going off to E. for a business venture which will add one or two million to the value of his estate: another meeting with heirs. Departure for E., abduction of Jamet by a rival party; he is going to be hanged as a spy. The said party is put to flight; and Jamet is going to be hanged, as mentioned already, executed by the vanquished. Flight, and embarkation at F.—sea sickness, famine, shipwreck. The captain is an heir, and declares with certainty that he has visited a church bearing the name 'St Colette the Hip-Swayer'—capture of the vessel by pirates. Injuries to M. Jamet's bottom. Arrival in America. Meeting of heirs or of families. As it is expected that M. Opime will be found in the north, a caravan heads off through the prairies. The Rocky Mountains. The continuation of M. Jamet's search throughout the whole country. Loss of an ear, attempt on a [] of M. Jamet. Return to Europe, end of the adventures of the Opime inheritance.

[Second page attached to manuscript]

Opime

M. Romauld Tertullien businessman based in Rotterdam

His older brother was one Vilfrid Romuald Tertullien

There had been several Tertullien families

The Carolus Tertulliens. The [ ] < ? > Tertulliens, and the Romuald Tertulliens

One of the heads of the Carolus family, following some bad business deals, had left The Hague and had gone to seek his fortune in a foreign land—there, as a simple soldier, he had enlisted under the banner of Washington and had also valiantly fought for the independence of the United States of America.

La Fayette had given to him [ ]

But his family had gone down in the world, had become ruined, and had spread, and had become practically lost in the mists of time.

○

Contributors

A ll who have contributed to this volume share in the statement made at the beginning of Jules Verne's 1904 novel, *Maître du monde* (*Master of the World*), when its narrator, John Strock, remarks, "If I speak of myself in this story, it is because I have been deeply involved in its startling events...."

Edward Baxter is a graduate of Mount Allison University and the University of Toronto, and has also studied at the University of Lausanne. He taught French for nearly thirty years at Ontario secondary schools, and was Head of Modern Languages at Don Mills Collegiate Institute in North York from 1977 until retiring in 1986. In 1980 he was appointed for a one-year term as the first Poet Laureate to the City of North York. Baxter has translated several hundred articles for the *Dictionary of Canadian Biography*, along with eight books. These include two distinguished new versions of Verne's *Family Without a Name* (1982) and *The Fur Country* (1987), both sponsored under the auspices of the Canada Council, published by the New Canada Press. Baxter's Afterword to the present volume first appeared in Brian Taves and Stephen Michaluk, Jr., *The Jules Verne Encyclopedia* (Scarecrow Press, 1996), and for that book Baxter also translated "The Humbug." He subsequently contributed a series of new Verne translations for several publishers: *The Invasion of the Sea* (Wesleyan, 2001), *The Golden Volcano* (Nebraska, 2008), and the 1882 play *Journey Through the Impossible* (2003), copublished by Prometheus and the North

American Jules Verne Society. Baxter has completed Verne's *The Count of Chanteleine* and other stories for the Palik Series.

Jean-Michel Margot is an internationally recognized specialist on Jules Verne. He currently serves as president of the North American Jules Verne Society and has published several books and many articles on Verne and his work. His most recent include a study of Verne's theatrical play *Journey Through the Impossible* (Prometheus, 2003), a volume of the 19thcentury Verne criticism title *Jules Verne en son temps* (Encrage, 2004) and the introduction and notes of Verne's *The Kip Brothers* (Wesleyan University Press, 2007).

Walter James Miller, television and radio writer, critic, poet, and translator, is one of the leading Verne scholars. His more than sixty books include *Engineers as Writers, Making an Angel: Poems*; critical commentaries on Vonnegut, Heller, Doctorow, and Beckett, and critical editions of Homer, Shakespeare, Conrad, Dickens, and Dumas. His articles, poems, and reviews have appeared in *The New York Times, New York Quarterly, Western Humanities Review, Literary Review, Explicator, College English, Authors Guild Bulletin, Science Fiction & Fantasy Book Review, Engineer, Transactions on Engineering Writing and Speech, Civil Engineering*, and many other periodicals and anthologies. From the *Literary Review* he has won its Charles Angoff Award for Excellence in Poetry; from the Armed Forces Service League, a prize for military fiction; and from the Engineers' Council for Professional Development, a special award for his NBC-TV series, *Master Builders of America*. A veteran of World War II, he is now Professor of English Emeritus at New York University.

CDs of four of Walter's radio broadcasts on Verne are available from the North American Jules Verne Society at www.najvs.org/audio.

Kieran O'Driscoll has recently been awarded his Ph.D. in Verne literary translation, by Dublin City University. His doctoral thesis was entitled *Around the World in Eighty Changes: A diachronic study of six complete translations (1873-2004), from French to English, of Jules Verne's novel, Le Tour du Monde en Quatre-Vingts Jours (1873)*, with the monograph version to be titled *Retranslation Through the Ages: The Example of Jules Verne*. This thesis explores the multiple causes of Verne retranslations.

Kieran holds a B.A. in Applied Languages (French and Spanish) with International Marketing Communications (2003) from Waterford Institute of Technology, and an M.A. in Translation Studies (2005) from Dublin City University, both degrees with First Class Honours. His Master's dissertation focused on the translations into French of J.K. Rowling's Harry Potter series. He has lectured in French at third-level, and in Advanced English as a Foreign Language, and has also done professional literary translation. Before entering academia, Kieran worked for almost twenty years in Irish local government, and also holds academic qualifications in Public Administration, Law and Music (Pianoforte).

Brian Taves (Ph.D., University of Southern California) has been an archivist with the Motion Picture/Broadcasting/Recorded Sound Division of the Library of Congress since 1990. He is the author of well over 100 articles, 25 chapters in anthologies, in addition to books on P.G. Wodehouse and Hollywood; on fantasy-adventure writer Talbot Mundy, in addition to editing an original anthology of Mundy's best stories; on the genre of historical adventure movies; and on director Robert Florey. In 2002-2003, Taves was chosen as Kluge Staff Fellow at the Library to write the first book on silent film pioneer Thomas Ince. Taves's writing on Verne has been translated into French, German, and Spanish, and he is writing a book on the 300 film and television adaptations of Verne worldwide. Taves is coauthor of *The Jules Verne Encyclopedia* (Scarecrow, 1993), and edited the first English-language publication of Verne's *Adventures of the Rat Family* (Oxford, 1993).

Acknowledgements

Peter Overstreet modified one of the orginal covers from the first French Hetzel editions of Jules Verne for this book. A professional Illustrator for two decades, he is director of "Legion Fantastique," the world's only Jules Verne re-enactment society.

Thanks to **Mark Eckell** for providing assistance with proofreading.

The Palik Series, while spearheaded by the **North American Jules Verne Society,** represents a cooperative effort among Vernians worldwide, pooling the resources and knowledge of the various organizations in different countries.

We are particularly grateful to **Bernhard Krauth**, chairman of the German Jules-Verne-Club since 2005. A deep sea licensed master working today as a docking pilot in Bremerhaven, Germany, Bernhard has published several articles in relation to Verne in France, the Netherlands and Germany. Intensely interested in the illustrations of the original French editions of Verne's work, he has been deeply involved in a project to digitize all of the illustrations, more than 5,000 in all. The project is for common, non-commercial use, and nearly all of the illustrations in this publication were made possible through his generosity.

○

The Palik Series

The last two decades have brought astonishing progress in the study of Jules Verne, with many new translations of Verne stories, even with the discovery of many new texts that had not been known before. Still there remain a number of Verne stories that have been overlooked, and it is this gap which the North American Jules Verne Society seeks to fill in the Palik series.

Through the generosity of our late member, Edward Palik, and the pooling of expertise by a variety of Verne scholars and translators around the world, we will be able to bring to the Anglophone public a series of hitherto unknown Verne tales.

Ed Palik had a special enthusiasm for bringing neglected Verne stories to English-speaking readers, and this will be reflected in the series that bears his name. In this way the society hopes to fulfill the goal that Ed's consideration has made possible. The volumes published will reveal the amazing range of Verne's storytelling, in genres that may astonish those who only know his most famous stories. We hope to allow a better appreciation of the famous writer who has, for more than a century and a half, been the widest-read author of fiction in the world.

CPSIA information can be obtained at www.ICGtesting.com
Printed in the USA
236879LV00007B/40/P